CONTENTS

CONTENTS

1 What is Cognitive Development?

KEY AIMS: By the end of Part 1 you will be able to:
▷ *define the nature and scope of cognitive development*
▷ *explain the relationship between intelligence and cognitive development in the context of the nature/nurture debate*
▷ *provide a brief overview of the three principal theoretical approaches to cognitive development.*

It seems obvious that cognitive development should be about the development of cognition, of how children come to understand the world around them and eventually become active participants in, and contributors to, the developing entity that is human civilization. Cognition covers a range of mental activities such as paying attention, learning and remembering, listening, speaking, thinking. Yet theories of cognitive development have a great deal to say about the development of thinking and knowledge — in short, intellectual development — and rather little about the growth of other cognitive processes.

Intelligence and cognitive development

One reason why cognitive development has taken on a somewhat specialized meaning has to do with psychology's traditional approach to intelligence. Initially, intelligence was thought to be a property that could be measured, like height or weight. Measurement, of course, was a complex procedure because human intelligence is made up of a variety of mental abilities; nevertheless, in principle, it was believed that a person's overall mental capacity could be 'captured' by administering a series of tests.

Nature *versus* nurture

An issue that has become almost inseparably attached to intelligence is that of the relative roles of **nature** and **nurture**. Put briefly, the central question is whether intelligence is inherited through the genes directly from parents (nature) or acquired through learning and experience (nurture). A moment's thought will tell you that this is an impossible question to answer, since human organisms are influenced by both genes and environment from the moment of conception. (*For further discussion of this see the companion Unit*, Aspects of Human Development.)

Think of your own intellectual preferences — the characteristic ways in which you solve problems, for instance. In what ways are these similar to, or different from, other members of your family? What might this mean?

Nature *and* nurture

An alternative view is to assume that intelligence is both a biological *and* an environmental phenomenon and one that is not easy to **operationalize** and measure. Instead much may be learned about the nature of intelligence by examining the development from its origins in infancy through to maturity with sophisticated abilities like problem-solving, logical analysis and reasoning. This is the position adopted by a Swiss psychologist, Jean Piaget, who devoted his long life to trying to answer the question: 'What is it about human beings — clearly *biological* organisms — that enables them to go way beyond the capabilities of all

1

other biological organisms to pose questions about the nature of truth, beauty, justice and, indeed, their own destiny?' Piaget, despite much criticism, remains the most influential figure not just in cognitive development but in developmental psychology as a whole.

There are three other major theories of cognitive development. One is linked to another important figure, the Russian, Lev Vygotsky, whose approach is referred to as **social constructivist**. As we shall see, there are a number of similarities between Piaget and Vygotsky, but whereas Piaget put his emphasis on children actively constructing their understanding of the world for themselves, Vygotsky saw development more as a partnership between the child and significant environmental agents such as parents and teachers. The role of language and instruction, relatively neglected by Piaget, is central to Vygotsky's view of cognitive development.

FIGURE 1: Fishing can be an individual or joint activity. Here, grandfather and child adopt a Vygotskian approach!

A figure who stands roughly midway between Piaget and Vygotsky, Jerome Bruner, represents a third theoretical position — one containing some original contributions and with a special interest in the applications of their work.

The fourth and final approach is not identified with any one individual and is popularly known as the information processing approach. Seeing human beings as systems which detect, register, process and evaluate, and then react appropriately to information that is being received, often simultaneously through a variety of channels, this approach reflects the influence of communications engineers and others who work in information technology.

Starting with a relatively simple information processor, such as the telephone, we can examine the sort of factors which affect its functioning (intensity of signal, number of competing signals, and so on) and draw profitable comparisons with humans. For instance, we know that our capacity for dealing with information is limited; like machines, if you overload us, we malfunction and the sort of errors we make throws light on how cognition works. If we add age as a factor, to observe what changes take place with time in information processing capacity, we begin to have an alternative conception of cognitive development.

SAQ
1

Which theoretical position — Piaget's, Vygotsky's, Bruner's or the information processing approach — is best represented in each of the following statements?
1. In order to understand the mind we need to look not only at the individual child but also at the education of that child.
2. Language, which is a social activity, plays a central role in intellectual development.
3. The capacity of human beings to make sense of the material that is constantly bombarding them is finite.
4. Intelligence is best understood by charting its development from origins in infancy to fruition in the mature organism.

What other artefacts, like the telephone, might shed light on information processing by human beings?

2 Jean Piaget (1896 — 1980)

> **KEY AIMS**
> ▷ To *acquaint you with Piaget's theory and outline the features of the cognitive developmental approach.*
> ▷ To *explain the psychological mechanisms that Piaget put forward to explain cognitive growth.*
> ▷ To *describe Piaget's four main stages of intellectual development.*
> ▷ To *show how these stages characterize children's thinking from infancy to adolescence.*
> ▷ To *summarize the main strengths of, and objections to, Piaget's theory.*

Jean Piaget had a working life of over 60 years and in that time he published 80 books and over 500 journal articles; he produced something like 25000 published pages of research and theory. You will not be expected to read it all! Fortunately, there is no shortage of introductions to Piaget's work (see Further Reading) and my aim here is only to provide an overview.

Piaget was a biologist interested in *epistemology* — the study of knowledge. He offered an alternative to the traditional armchair philosophers' approach to the age old question: 'How do we come to know what we know?' This was an empirical approach, namely an investigation of the child's development of knowledge. As a postgraduate just after World War I he trained in two areas of psychology that were then influential — **psychoanalysis** and mental testing. From psychoanalysis he learned the art of the clinical interview which he adapted for use with children. Many of Piaget's most powerful insights came from simply observing and talking to children about their understanding of **concepts**.

Piaget also worked in Paris in the laboratory of Alfred Binet, inventor of the intelligence test. Here, perhaps the most important thing he learned was that wrong answers to questions, in tests of reasoning for instance, are more informative about the child's underlying cognitive structures and understanding than correct answers. For example, to hear that the answer to the sum 10 + 10 is '20' tells you nothing except that the child knows how to do simple arithmetic or that he or she has guessed luckily. If the answer that is given is '11', however, you now begin to have some insights into the working of that child's mind, particularly if you follow it up with some judicious questioning.

FIGURE 2: Jean Piaget

Piaget's theory: The cognitive developmental approach

Piaget's approach, which has been widely adopted, is known as the cognitive developmental approach. It is marked by the following features:

1. In order to understand complex notions like thought, memory and language it is best to study the development of these systems from their earliest appearance in infancy.

2. Development proceeds by way of qualitative changes called, by Piaget, **stages**. Such development is not a steady accretion of skills but a series of rather sudden leaps. Each stage grows out of an earlier one and is a *reconstruction* of earlier knowledge. The result is a new way of looking at the world. Stages have common properties, which show themselves in the way a child tackles cognitive tasks, and they appear in the same order in all children.

3. Children are active contributors to their own cognitive growth, not passive organisms to be shaped only by rewards and punishments. This active, child-centred focus gives rise to the term **constructivist theory**: the child is thought continually to be 'constructing' an understanding of the world.

4. At the same time this approach is interactionist, not nativist. Psychological growth is not simply an unfolding of a predetermined plan but is dependent on a reciprocal, mutually dependent interaction between people and their environments. Thus, the child influences parents who further influence the child who then affects the parents, and so on.

5. So, how do children and adults develop and change? The mechanism for change is essentially *conflict*. All organisms that are capable of adapting to their environment are said to have a built-in tendency to seek equilibrium both within themselves and between themselves and their environments. In human beings, this entails continually resolving problems and conflicts that may arise because of a mismatch between one's mental view of the world and how it actually is. Piaget called this process **equilibration** which refers to a state of change (not a steady state, as the word might suggest).

Changing and developing: the adaptation model

Piaget's background in biology is evident in his adaptation model of intellectual growth. He believed that cognitive functioning is part of our genetic make-up. These inbuilt features of intelligent activity are **adaptation** and **organization** and they are present in all organisms that are capable of adapting to their environment.

The basic unit in the adaptation model is the organism *within* its environment (not the organism *and* its environment). From the start, the organism and the environment are seen as intimately related. From birth the organism has certain ways of orientating itself and behaving towards the environment, such as simple reflexes, which provide a framework for environmental events. At the same time, the environment is organized, in time and space, and this provides a setting for the activities of the organism. Thus each influences the other.

Can you think of any reflexes that a baby is born with?

Assimilation and accommodation. Adaptation is made up of two complementary processes: **assimilation** and **accommodation**. The organism utilizes something from its environment and *assimilates* it into existing **structures**. In Piaget's system structures are mental operations — ways of acting upon the world. Initially, in the young baby, these are simple procedures like looking and reaching but later they develop into complex logical operations like multiplication. With assimilation, therefore, the input is moderated or changed to fit the available ways of thinking.

Accommodation is the complementary process of adapting to demands from the outside. Note that we never get *pure* assimilation or *pure* accommodation — adaptation is a unitary event and both assimilation and accommodation are involved in any encounter with the environment. For example, at this moment, in reading about Piaget's adaptation model you are assimilating the material to your existing knowledge of psychology and biology. This helps you to make sense of what you are encountering. At the same time there will have to be some accommodation since some of the terms, and some of the ideas, are likely to be new to you. For instance, the word 'accommodation' itself has an everyday meaning to do with housing. If you simply assimilated the term to this meaning you would fail to understand the significance of the term for Piaget's theory. Cognitive progress is often a case of getting the assimilation/accommodation balance right.

FIGURE 3: This baby seems to have adapted to the demands of a spoon

To take another example from a much earlier stage of development: when babies are weaned from the breast or bottle to solid food, one of the experiences they must adapt to is taking food from a spoon rather than from a nipple. They can assimilate the new situation to the behaviour which has served them in the past, namely sucking, but sucking is not quite appropriate to taking food from a spoon. Learning to take food directly from a spoon takes a lot of practice — the lip and tongue movements required are quite different. There has to be some accommodation both to the object from which the food comes and to the texture of the food itself. In doing this, the infant can be said to have made some cognitive progress by developing a new scheme to cope with a new situation.

Explain the difference between assimilation and accommodation.

Cognitive structures are not static but continually developing. The infant has different structures from those of the child. Piaget's purpose — his life's work indeed — was to describe the essential features of structures which typify different levels of intellectual development and to explain the process by which structures develop out of one another.

Can you think of other examples of new cognitive structures that the infant acquires during the the first few months?

Schemes and operations. When talking of structures, Piaget more often refers to **schemes** and **operations**. In infants schemes refer to overt actions such as sucking and grasping. In later life they are internalized, highly organized actions called operations. Examples of these are logical rules such as classification and relation. But to say that grasping, for instance, is a scheme is to suggest that grasping is not a random activity but a predisposition to act on the world by repeatedly grasping objects and acquiring knowledge in this way. Similarly a logical scheme, like 'implication', will be applied repeatedly to different problems, such as: If A is bigger than B and B is bigger than C, then A must be bigger than C. The conclusion follows from the first two premises, logically, without having to be checked empirically. We have an extensive repertoire of such schemes and operations which we use to regulate exchanges with the external environment.

Describe three central components of Piaget's cognitive developmental approach.

Piaget's Method

Piaget set great store by giving his researchers a year's intensive training in the art of interviewing and experimenting with children. Initially, Piaget relied on observation and asking children straightforward questions about their understanding of the physical world. Later, he revised this method by presenting concrete objects or enacting events in front of the children who were required to respond by manipulating objects, not simply verbalizing. As Piaget recognized, the special skill in being an effective child researcher lies partly in being sufficiently flexible in questioning to follow the child's cognitive activity. In particular, opposing arguments are often needed to test the strength of the child's conviction.

A POSSIBLE PROJECT

If you have access to young children* (4—6 years), try to see what insights can be obtained into their thinking by asking them to tell you what they think dreams are; why clouds move; what is a friend; why does water disappear when you heat it — where does it go, etc. (*You should seek advice from your tutor before tackling work of this sort. It is important to know how to go about talking to children, establishing rapport with them and respecting their rights and best interests. It is also important for reasons of their safety, initially to approach the Head Teacher of the school or nursery to explain what you are trying to achieve.)

Stages of intellectual development

Piaget's is a stage-dependent theory. This does not mean that the stages represent inborn **maturational** processes; there is no fixed timetable, but the order of their appearance is invariable. The stages refer to the state of the structures (thought processes) available to the child at any particular time. They do not refer to the store of knowledge possessed by the child but to the nature of the cognitive system. As we shall see, this develops from beginnings that are largely limited to overt actions — grasping, sucking and crying — through a period that is very much determined by external perceptual events — for example, the failure to realize that the amount of liquid in a glass does not change when it is poured into a different shaped glass — to a point, in late adolescence, when problem solving is increasingly under the control of rational modes of thinking.

There are four main stages: **sensorimotor, pre-operational, concrete operational** and **formal operational**. There are also dozens of intermediate substages related to particular concepts such as time, causality, number, space and even dreams and morality. At any one time, the child may be at different stages in different areas.

Stage 1. Sensorimotor period (0–2 years)

This stage covers roughly the first two years of life during which the infant achieves the highest level of intelligence possible without the assistance of (later developing) symbolic processes such as language. Babies demonstrate their intelligence in the way in which they deal with objects and events using every means available to them such as looking, reaching, grasping and sucking. This is a vital stage because later, more advanced forms of reasoning have their beginnings in these overt sensorimotor responses.

This first stage is further divided into six substages.

☐ (i)   For the first month of life the infant is restricted to exercising and refining innate reflexes such as sucking.

☐ (ii) The second substage (1—4 months), *primary circular reactions*, features pleasurable responses centred on the child's own body, discovered by chance, and performed over and over again. Sucking, for example, may begin with the nipple and move to the fingers. Thumb-sucking is a familiar primary circular reaction.

☐ (iii) *Secondary circular reactions* (4—8 months) are also pleasurable events that stimulate their own repetition but this time they centre on objects and events in the external environment, for example, shaking a rattle.

☐ (iv) The fourth substage, *co-ordination of secondary circular reactions* (8—12 months) marks the beginning of intentional behaviour. For example, the child will combine lifting and grasping schemes to achieve a goal such as moving a cushion out of the way to get at a toy.

☐ (v) The fifth substage, *tertiary circular reactions* (12—18 months) sees the infant experimenting with objects to create interesting outcomes. Dropping objects out of the pram repeatedly (different objects, different surfaces, different heights, and so on) to see the reaction (both on the objects and on adults!) is a familiar example.

☐ (vi) The final substage, *inner experimentation* (18—24 months), is where the infant begins to construct internal representations, such as images, and marks the transition into the pre-operational phase of thought. (These stages are further illustrated in Box 1 which examines the development of the object concept, one of Piaget's most famous discoveries.)

BOX 1. The development of the object concept

When I put a pen away in my inside pocket I would be surprised if it wasn't there when I next reached for it. We take it for granted that objects have an existence independent of our perception of them. Piaget showed that this capacity is not inborn — the idea that objects exist when they are out of sight has a developmental history of at least 18 months corresponding to the six substages we have already outlined.

0—4 months (SUBSTAGES 1 and 2): An infant is playing with a toy when it is taken and hidden from view. The infant makes no attempt to look for the object — it is as if the object ceased to exist.

4—8 months (SUBSTAGE 3): If the object is partially hidden, the infant will search for it. But no search will be made for a completely hidden object even though the infant saw where it was concealed.

8—12 months (SUBSTAGE 4): The infant will now search for and retrieve an object which he or she saw being hidden. But if, after successfully finding an object in one place on a number of occasions, the infant sees the object moved to a new hiding place, he or she will look only in the first hiding place. This is known as the 'place error'.

BOX 1. *continued*

12—18 months (SUBSTAGE 5): Infants will now look for objects in a variety of locations as long as they have seen them being moved. But if someone pretends to hide an object in one place (under a pillow) and then moves the hand containing the concealed object to another location (a box), the infant will look only under the pillow.

18—24 months (SUBSTAGE 6): Infants will now continue to search for objects even if they have been secretly hidden. They enjoy playing hiding games themselves and show that they have a **representation** of objects — they know that they must continue to exist somewhere.

Stage 2. Pre-operational period (2–6 years)

This stage covering the preschool period is marked by the acquisition of new and remarkable skills. Around their second birthday children come to use language, to pretend, and to have dreams and nightmares. All these demonstrate that the child can understand symbols, like the sound 'cat' to mean the four-legged furry creature that the toddler chases. This symbolic function allows the child to understand references to objects or events even in their absence. For example, a mother can ask her child if he or she wants a drink and be understood even though the physical object 'drink' is not present.

Language is the most obvious set of symbols and is particularly powerful because it is socially shared. But there are also other symbolic forms like mental images, pictures and pretend play. Note that for Piaget language, although powerful, is not the only form of thought and developmentally it *follows* other forms.

The huge advantage of symbols is that they allow thought to be separated from action. Just think about this. In particular it provides *speed* in representing a long series of actions, *liberation* from the immediate situation, and *simultaneous* represent-ation of related elements. To pursue the earlier example of the drink and the various actions involved — taking the juice from the fridge, putting it in a beaker, possibly adding some water — these can all be reduced to one mental event. And, as a mental rather than a physical operation, it can happen in a flash. As for liberation, the child can consider what is entailed in the question: 'Do I want a drink?'; 'What sort of drink would I like?'; 'Do I want a biscuit as well?' All of this is done without any sensorimotor action, such as holding up the cup, which was necessary at the earlier stage. If the sensorimotor child's mental functioning is likened to a series of slide projections, then the pre-operational child has full movie projection capability. But pre-operational thinking is still immature in a number of ways which I will explain in more detail.

SAQ
4

What are the main differences between the way an eighteen-month-old and a three-year-old will play with an adult?

(i) **Transductive reasoning**. Adults generally reason either from the general to the particular, which we call *deduction*, or from the particular to the general (*induction*). Pre-operational children will often reason from the particular to the particular so that if A is like B in one respect, it is assumed that it must be like B in all respects. Piaget gives the example of his daughter Lucienne who regularly took a nap in the afternoon. On one occasion, when she did not take a nap, she said, 'I haven't had my nap so it isn't afternoon'. Her thought had moved from one particular (the nap) to another particular (the afternoon) and made the unwarranted assumption that one depended on the other.

(ii) **Centration**. This is the tendency to centre attention on one aspect or detail of a situation with an apparent inability to shift attention or to include other relevant features. A good example of this is the conservation task (see Box 2). O'Bryan and Boersma (1971) provided convincing evidence of this by filming children's eye movements while they were engaged in a conservation of liquid task. Figure 4 shows that children who do not understand that the amount of liquid is not affected by the shape of the container (non-conservers) will concentrate their attention on the most powerful perceptual cue — the height of the juice in the glass — and ignore the logical fact that nothing has been added to or taken away from the amount. In contrast 'conservers' will attend almost equally to relevant features in both containers.

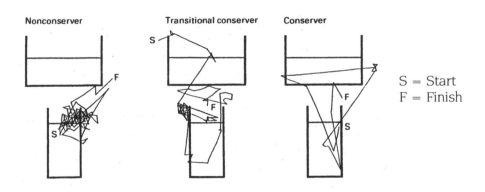

FIGURE 4.: In these records of eye movement scan paths, note how the non-conserver (on the left) centres on one salient point while the conserver (on the right) takes relevant information economically from both vessels. (After O'Bryan and Boersma (1971). *Journal of Experimental Child Psychology*, 12.)

BOX 2. The conservation problem

Adults are often surprised to learn that young children believe that the amount of plasticine in a ball is changed if that ball is worked into a different shape, such as a 'pancake' or 'sausage'. The ability to recognize that quantities remain the same in spite of irrelevant transformations is the essence of the conservation problem. It was Piaget who demonstrated that it had a developmental history. It is a phenomenon that can be investigated for many dimensions including mass, number, length, area, weight and volume.

The procedure for a variety of conservation tasks is illustrated below. The essential idea is that first you make sure that the child judges that two amounts are equal, such as two identical glasses of orange juice. Then you alter one of the amounts in some way by, for example, pouring one of the drinks into a taller, thinner glass, and ask if there is just as much drink in one glass as there is in the other. The pre-operational (non-conserving) child will say that they are not the same and will often point to one of the glasses as having more. A child who says they remain the same is a conserver. However, for Piaget to grant this status, the child would have to explain his or her answer by supporting it with a logical statement such as, 'Because you haven't added or taken anything away, it must still be the same'.

Type of Conservation	Child sees	Experimenter then transforms display	Child is asked conservation question
Length	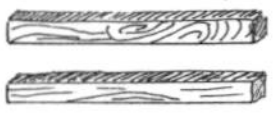 Two sticks of equal length and agrees that they are of equal length.	 Moves stick over.	Which stick is longer? Preconserving child will say that one of the sticks is longer. Conserving child will say that they are both the same length.
Liquid quantity	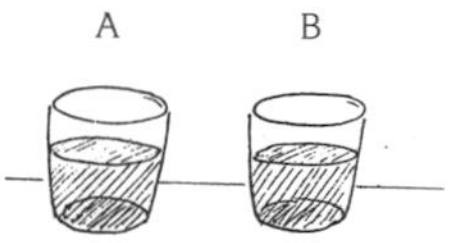 Two beakers filled with water and says that they both contain the same amount of water.	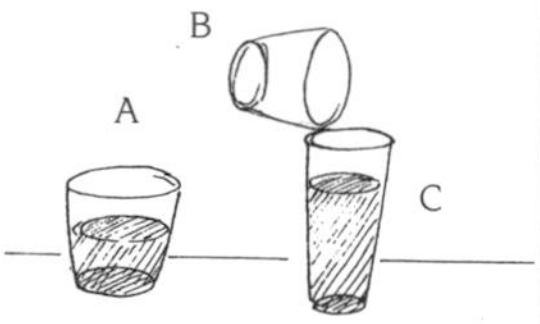 Pours water from B into a tall, thin beaker C, so that water level in C is higher than in A.	Which beaker has more water? Preconserving child will say C has more water: "See, it's higher." Conserving child will say that they have the same amount of water: "You only poured it!".
Substance amount	 Two identical clay balls and acknowledges that the two have equal amounts of clay.	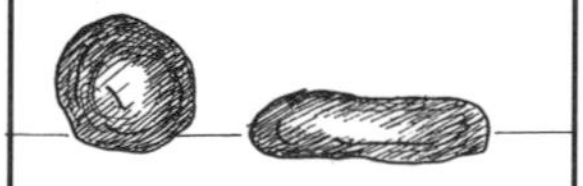 Rolls out one of the balls.	Do the two pieces have the same amount of clay? Preconserving child will say that the long piece has more clay. Conserving child will say that the two pieces have the same amount of clay.

The conservation task has been replicated many times, but controversy surrounds the explanation for success and failure. Explanations in terms of attention, memory, language and social factors have been put forward and it is clear that the precise circumstances under which the task is presented does affect the result (Donaldson, 1978).

FIGURE 5

(iii) **Egocentrism**. One of Piaget's early discoveries was that young children often reason from the standpoint that their view of the world is the only one. This can be demonstrated in several ways. In the famous 'Three Mountains Experiment' Piaget asked children to look at a model of typical Swiss mountain terrain. This is illustrated in Figure 6 and you will see that according to the point from which you view the object, so the foreground, background and left and right landmarks will change. This point was not understood by pre-operational children who were asked to select pictures which showed either their own viewpoint (point A on the diagram) or those of a doll which had been placed at other points (B or C). They tended to choose the picture that matched their own. Piaget called this an egocentric bias and he demonstrated that **egocentrism** permeates pre-operational thinking. Using a different example, Piaget found that when questioning children about their notion of 'foreigners', there was no doubt in the Swiss children's minds that the French were foreigners. What they would not admit was that the Swiss were foreigners to the French!

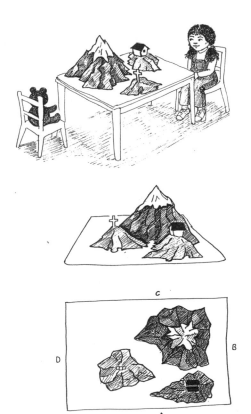

FIGURE 6: The three-mountains task challenges the young child's ability to take an alternative perspective

(iv) **States versus transformations**. The pre-operational child tends to focus on successive states rather than on the transformations by which change comes about. The **conservation** task is a good example of this. If we start with the same number of counters in one to one correspondence (Figure 7,situation A), it is not difficult to respond that they are the same. But when one line is then spread out (situation B), any inclination to ignore the way in which the change took place — the transformation procedure — is likely to lead to a false judgement about number and, of course, a failure to conserve. It is by knowing about transformations, and not being restricted to before and after states, that adults can cope with changes in perceptual appearance. This is a principal reason why children are so gullible to disappearing tricks, conjuring tricks and the like. A further illustration of this notion can be found in the following Something to Try task.

Situation A   Situation B

FIGURE 7

SOMETHING TO TRY

If you have access to a three- or four-year-old try the following task. Show the child a pencil standing up vertically. Then push the pencil over so that it lies horizontally. Now give the child a sheet of paper and a pencil and ask him or her to draw the pencil at different points as it moves from the standing to the lying position. Alternatively, create a series of simple drawings yourself showing the pencil at the start and finish point and also intermediate orientations on its way down. Ask the child to pick out, from the drawings, the intermediate points as the pencil makes its journey from vertical to horizontal. If Piaget is right, you will find that children ignore the intermediate positions.

(v) **Reversibility**. By now you may have realized that all these different features of the pre-operational child's thought are interrelated. They are due to the rigidity of the child's thought, its stimulus-bound nature in the sense that events in the outer world carry much more force than the developing, internal world of mental concepts. Piaget's favourite way of contrasting pre- and operational stages is by looking at the extent to which any thought pattern is reversible. All mathematical or logical operations, for example, are reversible:

$$4 + 3 = 7; 7 - 3 = 4$$

And in terms of verbal propositions: All boys and all girls = all children
                                      All children except all girls = all boys

Pre-operational children cannot follow this kind of reasoning.

SAQ
5

Read the dialogue below and consider in what ways it illustrates the nature of pre-operational thinking.
Adult: What is your name?
Child: Sam.
Adult: Do you have a brother?
Child: Yes, George.
Adult: Does George have a brother?
Child: No.

SAQ
6

What does the term 'conservation' mean?

Stage 3. Concrete operational stage (7–11 years)

This stage characterizes the primary school years and provides a much more stable and integrated system of thinking. Piaget sees operations as essentially mental actions with logico-mathematical properties and the big advantage is that children are no longer at the mercy of their perceptions. They are decentered and able to conserve quantity across irrelevant transformations, for instance.

It is in this period that the child begins to grasp that objects can be put into categories (or classes) and that these categories have relations between them. Toy bricks, for example, may have the *same* shape but be of a different *size* and *colour*. This gives the overall class of, say, cubes and the subclasses of big ones and small ones which can be further subdivided into big, black ones and big, white ones, and so on.

FIGURE 8. Are there more daffodils or more flowers?

A well known Piagetian task that illustrates the difference between operational and pre-operational children is known as the 'class inclusion' problem. The children are shown a bunch of flowers made up of four tulips and ten daffodils (Figure 8). All children will tell you that these are all flowers and that there are more daffodils than tulips. If asked, however, if there are more daffodils or more flowers, pre-operational children will respond, 'more daffodils'. They fail to sort out the part — whole relationship between flowers and daffodils — they appear not to realize that one class (flowers) can include another (daffodils). It seems that the pre-operational child is unable to consider part and whole simultaneously. The concrete operational child, in contrast, is not centred on the more dominant of the two subclasses and is able to handle hierarchical classifications like this. As long as the problem is presented in a concrete way, using physical objects, quite complex hierarchies can be constructed. Presenting the problem in a purely verbal form, however, presents difficulties. Competence at this level is still to come.

As well as classes and categories there are also relations between objects. Objects can often be ordered in terms of dimensions like size, weight, brightness and so on. Like most cognitive skills this is also age-dependent. For instance, a child at a certain stage may be able to sort from big to little but not the other way round. He or she may be able to put a series of objects in order of height without error but when asked to insert some extra items in the appropriate places they will have considerable difficulty.

A POSSIBLE PROJECT

A number of the tasks referred to can be tried with children aged six to eight. For example, the class inclusion task might be done with sweets (such as Smarties and jelly babies). Try experimenting with the way in which you phrase the task. Can you improve performance by rewording the questions? Does it make any difference if you use physical objects or do the task verbally?

Stage 4. Formal operational stage (12 years and upwards)

According to Piaget this is the last developmental stage in which abstract thought finally emerges with complete decentering and reversibility. The person is now guided by the form of an argument and can ignore the content if they wish. (You may not believe in the paranormal, for example, but will be prepared to accept the premiss that extra sensory perception (ESP) exists in order to follow the logic of an argument about it.) Purely verbal problems such as: 'Edith is fairer than Susan; Edith is darker than Lily — who is the darkest?', that cause problems for the concrete operational child, can now be solved. (Think about it!) Formal operations provide access to a hypothetical world. It is one reason why adolescents enjoy theorizing and criticizing so much. They realize that the way things are is not inevitable; they could be different and perhaps better.

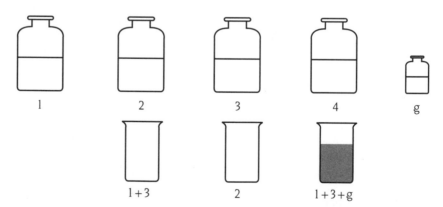

FIGURE 9: Materials for experiment on formal operational thinking. (After Inhelder and Piaget, 1958)

In sudying formal operations, Piaget and his colleagues asked people to try to solve scientific problems to see to what extent they used procedures such as the *hypothetico-deductive* method. An example of such a problem is illustrated in Figure 9. The person is given four flasks all with a similar amount of colourless liquid. Each flask contains a different chemical solution. A fifth flask contains an indicator, that is, a substance which signals (through a change in colour) that a chemical reaction has taken place. The person is then shown two glasses which also hold colourless, odourless solutions. The indicator is added to both glasses, one of which turns yellow. The person's task is to reproduce the colour using all or any of the five flasks. What is interesting, of course, is not so much the right answer (which could happen by chance) but the way in which the person sets about trying to achieve an answer. Do the participants operate like young scientists, testing hypotheses and discarding them when necessary, or do they use unsystematic trial and error?

So why is Piaget's theory still important?

☐ It is the most comprehensive account we have of the growth of children's thinking backed up with a wealth of ingenious experiments. At an **empirical** level the work is central and provides a benchmark against which to test current research.

☐ Piaget's structuralist approach seeks to integrate the range of psychological capabilities that exist at a given stage. Although there has been much criticism of his approach (some of which we will examine later), objections to bits of the theory do not demolish the theory as a whole.

☐ Piaget cannot easily be labelled a 'nativist' or 'environmentalist'. (Remember the nature versus nurture argument.) He is, rather, an 'interactionist'. He saw the influences of both maturation and environment as being mediated by the developing mind itself.

☐ Piaget's approach sees development as dependent on the child's active discovery of properties of the world. But this is not a ready-made external reality nor one of predetermined ideas. Knowledge is, rather, a construct which shows itself in the constant elaboration of new structures.

☐ The impact on education has been huge. The *Plowden Report* in 1967 recommended that schools in the UK, especially primary schools, should follow Piaget in advocating child-centred, discovery learning. Today there is some moderation of this view which we will consider in part 8.

☐ Piaget's stage-dependent approach has been criticized though the invariant order of the stages has not.

☐ Piaget has also been criticized for neglecting two things: the role of language and of social factors. This is a just criticism but he did not neglect them completely. He certainly believed that language plays a role in thinking, and he recognized the role of social processes in reducing egocentrism, particularly in areas such as morality and communication where social awareness is important.

☐ Towards the end of his career Piaget was increasingly concerned with the nature of consciousness — with the role of **metacognition**, thinking about thinking; the role of planning and monitoring one's own actions and understanding. This is an important area where a lot of research is currently being carried out and shows Piaget to have been in the vanguard to the end.

☐ The conclusion, therefore, is do not write off Piaget. You will come across plenty of criticism of his work and it is tempting to leave out the Swiss genetic epistemologist because his writings are not always easy to understand. Almost always, however, the effort is worthwhile.

What is meant by formal operational thought?

SOMETHING TO TRY

Try the following task with a number of students across the secondary school age range (say 11, 13 and 15 years). Give them a sheet of paper at the top of which are written the letters A E M S T. Ask them to see how many words they can make from these letters. A formal operational solution would be to use a systematic procedure that generates all the possible permutations. They might start, for instance, with all the two-letter words, followed by all those of three letters and so on. By following the workings on the page and comparing different strategies and different ages, you will be able to see the extent to which each student's thinking follows the principles of formal operational thought or is unsystematic and disorganized.

Social Constructivist Theory

KEY AIMS: By the end of Part 3 you will be acquainted with:

> ▷   the main themes and contributions of Vygotskian theory
> ▷   the link between culture, instruction and cognitive development
> ▷   the zone of proximal development and the notion of assisted learning
> ▷   the significance of egocentric speech in Vygotsky's theory and that of Piaget
> ▷   Vygotsky's experimental procedure and main findings in the investigation of children's thinking.

Piaget was criticized for his relative neglect of the role of social factors in cognitive development. In contrast, a theory which emphasizes social and cultural influences is that of the Russian psychologist, Lev Vygotsky. Although Vygotsky was an exact contemporary of Piaget, the latter outlived him by 46 years.

Lev Vygotsky (1896 — 1934)

Vygotsky first took a degree in law but then became a teacher of literature and carried out some early research on artistic creation. In 1924 he began serious work in the areas of child psychology, education and psychopathology, but died of tuberculosis ten years later at the age of 37. The political climate of post-revolutionary Russia is certainly important to an understanding of Vygotsky's work. He emphasized the importance of sociocultural factors in human cognitive development but was not a crude **determinist** — he did not believe that there was a simple causal relationship between environmental events and human responses. He rejected the doctrines of **behaviourism** and **introspection** which were fashionable at the time and, instead, stated that conscious thought processes were a proper study for psychology. His main focus was on thinking and speech, and he took an empirical and developmental approach.

FIGURE 10: Lev Vygotsky (Gratefully reproduced by permission of G.L. Vygodskaya and R.van der Veer)

Vygotsky's approach to cognitive development

Two very different definitions of intelligence underlie the thinking of these two major theorists, Piaget and Vygotsky.

1. Intelligence is the ability of the organism to adapt to its environment.

2. Intelligence is the capacity to learn through instruction.

Can you guess which describes Piaget's position and which Vygotsky's?

Both definitions refer to the individual and the environment but Piaget's (definition 1), through the adaptation model (which, of course, includes assimilation *and* accommodation) places more emphasis on the individual. The reference to instruction in Vygotsky's definition (definition 2) puts the emphasis on the environment.

Piaget tried to unify biology, the natural sciences and psychology. Vygotsky's aim was to integrate psychology with history, culture and sociology. In Vygotsky's system the role played by culture is important. Culture is manifested by systems of symbols — language, science, the media, and so on — and these influence the development of intelligence. To Vygotsky, these systems are not to be seen merely as the content of thinking, they are *part of its structure* and activity. The systems themselves have a dynamic structuring effect on learning and development. Language provides a way of construing and constructing the world; it is not just the labels we apply to it.

Both Piaget and Vygotsky stress the importance of action. For Piaget, action is typically individual and constructive. Vygotsky prefers the term *activity* with an intentionally stronger social dimension. To Vygotsky, activity begins in the external social world and is gradually **internalized** by the child to form a central feature of his or her intellectual processes. A clear advantage is seen for thought over direct action. It can be used as a substitute for real action; one can try out an action in the mind. Errors may be revealed at this stage and prevented before real enactment. In evolutionary terms, thought has obvious survival value: it saves energy, avoids dangers, and so on.

Let us take an all too familiar example. You might think that your best strategy for preparing for an examination is to put in a great deal of revision effort just before the exam so that everything will be fresh in your memory. But, on further reflection, you realize that the amount of work required needs more than a week or two and that a big effort might leave you exhausted, unable to give of your best. You may also decide that exam preparation is more than simply cramming; it requires you to think through issues, prepare outline answers, and so on. In such ways, thinking and planning help us to get the best out of ourselves!

Instruction and intelligence

Piaget was suspicious of the role of tuition and claimed that it led to the learning of procedures and not to the development of *understanding*. For example, it may be possible for students to gain good marks for an exam answer by recalling and presenting rote-learned facts, but if the theory that binds these facts together is not understood they have little intellectual merit. A more profound form of knowledge, according to Piaget, depends principally on the child's own unassisted efforts.

Vygotsky saw the capacity to learn through instruction as a fundamental feature of human intelligence. For him, the continuation of culture requires that the immature learn and the mature teach.

The zone of proximal development

Vygotsky coined the term **zone of proximal development** (ZPD) to refer to 'the level of potential development as determined through problem solving under adult guidance or in collaboration with more capable peers ... What children can do with the assistance of others might be in some sense even more indicative of their mental development than what they can do alone.' (Vygotsky, 1978: 87). Thus, something like a test situation, usually done individually, might not reveal the full potential of the child. Vygotsky's claim is that all developing individuals have both an *actual* developmental level and a ZPD. Both of these aspects need to be considered in any assessment of a child.

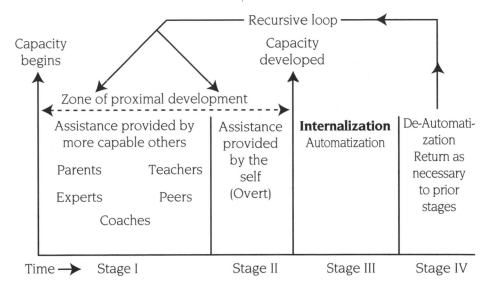

FIGURE 11: A Schematic representation of how ZPD might work over time via a series of stages (After Tharp and Gallimore, 1988).

If we think in terms of a particular capacity, say reading, a very young child is only able to read with considerable help by others. From the highly scaffolded Stage I (see Figure 11) the child moves into Stage II in which, increasingly, the child helps him or herself by, for example, reading aloud. This overt method of self- instruction also allows the supporter to intervene in case of trouble. Stages III and IV move outside the ZPD by which time everyday reading is an internalized and highly **automized** process. Note, however, that Stage IV allows the possibility of returning to the ZPD should it be required.

When first encountering something like a computer manual, for instance, you may understand it more easily if you read through the text with an expert offering guidance as to what particular terms mean. 'Co-operatively achieved success' — one of Vygotsky's phrases — is at the heart of Vygotsky's thinking.

What did Vygotsky mean by the 'zone of proximal development'?

Language and thought: speech and thinking

So what of the role of language? Piaget's view was that language is only one of the symbolic functions which develops *after* the sensorimotor period, along with images, **symbolic play** and drawing. Thought, therefore, precedes language and derives mainly from action; the importance of language is as the principal means by which we exchange ideas.

Vygotsky prefers the terms *speech* and *thinking* to language and thought, in line with his view of speech as a public and shared activity. He summarized his position as follows:

1.   In their development, thinking and speech have different roots.

2.   Initially there is a pre-intellectual stage for speech and a pre-linguistic stage for thought.

3.   Up to a certain point in time, the two follow different lines, independently of each other.

4.   At a certain point in development these lines meet, whereupon thought becomes verbal and speech rational.

5.   Thinking and speech never completely overlap; that is, there is nonverbal thought (for example, mental images) and there is nonconceptual speech (for example, rote repetition).

There is a lot to unravel here. The first three points are close to Piaget's position, but point four certainly is not, and this is where the two theories diverge sharply.

Egocentric speech: Piaget's view

In the discussion of Piaget's theory, reference was made to the notion of **egocentrism**, a characteristic of the pre-operational stage. A particular manifestation of this is egocentric speech, in which the child, in conversation, shows an inability to take account of others. The child is talking *at* others rather than *to* them. For Piaget, the development of this phenomenon can be summarized as follows:

presocial speech ➤➤ egocentric speech ➤➤ social speech

If, through egocentric speech, you are unable to take account of the perspective of others, it follows that communication will be difficult and intellectual cooperation almost impossible. What others say is assimilated to the child's own point of view, often distorting the meaning of what is said. It is only with the acquisition of operational thought (allowing **decentering**, reversibility, and so on), that egocentric speech drops away. Reciprocity and mutual understanding are not achieved until the concrete operational stage. Piaget believed the process is aided by social contact, especially with peers.

Egocentric speech: Vygotsky's view

For Vygotsky the progression is rather different:

global social speech ➤➤ egocentric speech ➤➤ inner speech
↖ communicative speech

According to Vygotsky, speech arises from a social need, and egocentric speech derives from this and has a different function, that of *self-guidance*. Initially, language is entirely a social activity which contrasts with Piaget's claim that sociability through language is unavailable to the young child. Vygotsky's position is that, at first, the child does not distinguish between speech for others and speech for self.

For example, three-year-old Nick is with a friend drawing and he chats while he is doing it:

'Gonna draw a man thing. A beard. Hair we need. Ears. Mouth here.'

Egocentric speech for Vygotsky is a hybrid form which has the structure of inner speech. It is **telegraphic** (abbreviated) but is vocalized as social speech. Nick's speech seems partly a commentary on what he is doing and partly a guide to his own activity. One feels that he would say these things whether his friend was with him or not. Egocentric speech does not decrease with age but rises in quantity and quality (the extent to which it becomes abbreviated) at about age seven. Then it submerges to become inner speech.

Inner speech: Vygotsky's view

Inner speech is something we all use. Often we are unaware of it, but in children it is more likely to come to the surface. Vygotsky pointed out that it is especially likely to occur if we are interrupted during an activity. An example comes from my own research (Lloyd, 1982) in which a four-year-old child was describing a picture, from a set of similar pictures of houses, to another child. On the basis of the description the listening child had to locate the target. The speaking child was interrupted in her activity by a distraction from the listening partner. She said: 'Stop it, Jamie, I've got to do this.' She then said 'colour first' quietly, but audibly, as if to herself and then produced her description: 'It's got a red roof, open windows and there's smoke coming from the chimney'. 'colour first' seems to be an example of inner speech, serving a **self-regulatory function** to help in the effective performance of the task. It has the classic properties of inner speech being telegraphic or abbreviated.

SOMETHING TO TRY

When you next find you are silently talking to yourself, think about why you are doing it. Is it, for example, just an accompaniment to thought or action or does it seem to be guiding what you are doing?

SAQ
9

What is meant by egocentrism?

Language and the zone of proximal development

A famous disciple of Vygotsky's, Alexander Luria, investigated the role played by speech in planning and controlling children's behaviour — the **regulatory function** of speech. This becomes particularly significant when combined with ZPD, since the regulative function of language is critical to cognitive growth. Imagine a parent or teacher helping a child in a problem-solving activity such as completing a puzzle or constructing a model. The internalization process — the movement from other-regulation to self-regulation — is as follows:

Stage I: The adult controls and guides the child's activity using verbal and nonverbal behaviour.

Stage II: Next, the adult and child come to share problem-solving functions, with the child increasingly taking the initiative and the adult correcting and guiding when the child falters.

Stage III: Finally, the adult cedes control to the child and now functions primarily as a supportive audience.

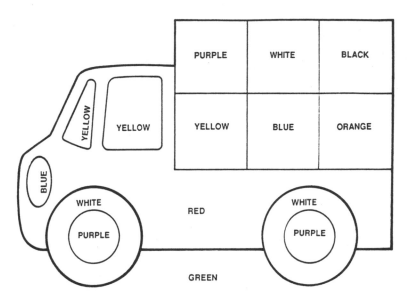

FIGURE 12: Jigsaw puzzle used in joint problem-solving task (Wertsch *et al.*, 1980).

Let's look in detail at a study of this process. Wertsch *et al.* (1980) asked mothers to help their preschool children to copy the model shown in Figure 12. It was found that, at Stage I, mothers did most of the talking, showing and telling the child what to do. By Stage II, during the course of the task, the mothers began to say less and the children began to say and do more. This was the beginning of the sharing phase. Increasingly mothers' instructions became abbreviated and the children decided what to do, accompanying their actions with appropriate language. Finally, by Stage III, if the partnership was successful, each mother was now just making the occasional comment or suggestion and their child was in control of the task. The language of both participants was increasingly abbreviated but it was noticeable that the child used speech to regulate his or her actions. The supposition is that, with increasing mastery, what is at first overt speech will become inner speech.

SAQ
10

Attribute the following statements to either Vygotsky or Piaget:
1. *Thought is internalized action.*
2. *Thought is internalized speech.*
3. *Changes in thinking result from activities mediated by an expert.*
4. *Thinking develops through active discovery.*
5. *Development passes through stages which are themselves reconstructions of earlier stages.*
6. *Development is a cultural phenomenon.*

SOMETHING TO TRY

Invent a small general knowledge quiz (about 20 questions) including questions about capitals of countries, names of rivers, famous buildings, historical events, the world of sport and the arts, etc. Try it out on a few people, administering it in two ways.

(1)   Simply ask the questions and note down the responses, including 'don't knows'.

(2)   Repeat the quiz, this time giving clues where the person has got the answer wrong first time e.g., mention the first letter, or first name.

What do the results tell you about the zone of proximal development?

BOX 3. Thinking in chain complexes

Unlike Piaget, Vygotsky conducted very few empirical investigations. The best known is a study of children's thinking. For this he used a set of wooden blocks of different colours, shapes, heights and sizes with no two blocks completely alike. Each block had a **nonsense word** written on the bottom surface (invisible to the child), such as 'miv'. These words represented four classes such as tall and large; short and small, etc. Some dimensions, in Vygotsky's case colour and shape, were 'irrelevant'. The blocks were spread in front of the child randomly and the tester turned over one of the blocks revealing the name. The child was asked to select the other blocks which might carry the same name. If the child 'guessed' wrongly, which was usually the case, the tester turned over one of the incorrect choices, pointed out that it did not have the right name on the bottom, and invited the child to try again. This process was repeated until the problem was solved or discontinued. Vygotsky's method is of more interest than the detailed findings which need not concern us. There is, however, a particular mode of children's thinking uncovered by this experiment which offers a very good example of a type of thinking to which preschool children are particularly prone. This is called thinking in complexes, the best known example being **chain complexes**.

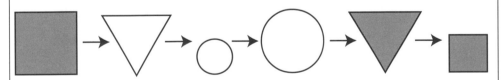

FIGURE 13: An example of a chain complex

An example of a chain complex is shown above. What distinguishes such solutions to a task like Vygotsky's is that though there is a meaningful bond between each item and the next in the sequence — at first the link is size, then it is colour, then it is form, etc — there is no such common property across the whole chain.   This shows that the child at this age is prey to short-term, associative links rather than a higher level approach to concepts that both analyses the features that discriminate one item from another and recognizes what it is that unites different things, using a process of synthesis. A child following such a strategy, therefore, would put a pile of blocks together that had a clear, common property (or properties), such as all the circular shapes or all the large, shaded ones.

FIGURE 14: This child is developing motor mastery with the reassurance of a supportive adult in attendance

4

Bruner's Contribution to Cognitive Development

KEY AIMS: By *the end of part 4 you should understand:*
▷ *Jerome Bruner's approach to representation*
▷ *the complementary roles played by evolution, perception, language and instruction in Bruner's system*
▷ *the similarities and differences in the theories of Bruner, Piaget and Vygotsky.*

Jerome Bruner has been the most influential American developmental psychologist for the past 30 years. His theoretical ideas draw on both Piaget and Vygotsky but he has also made a distinctive contribution of his own. Like Piaget, he believes that *action* is the starting place for the formation of abstract, symbolic thinking, but he rejects Piaget's emphasis on stages and logical operations. Like Vygotsky he values the role of instruction and social interaction in cognitive growth and this has had a major impact on educational policy in the United States.

Bruner's theory of representation

The way in which the external world of objects and events is created in the mind is known as **representation**. Like Piaget, Bruner believed that representation is affected by development and he pointed to three different modes of representation — **enactive, iconic** and **symbolic** — which he believed to be developmentally ordered. So, what exactly are these three modes?

Mode 1: **Enactive representation**. This mode refers to perceptual motor actions and is close to Piaget's sensorimotor schemes. But Bruner believes that it is not limited to infancy and is involved in many familiar activities like walking, driving and tying shoelaces. It can be considered as a practical intelligence where representation at a physical, muscular level is important.

FIGURE 15: Jerome Bruner

Mode 2: **Iconic representation**. Whenever we use our imagination to help us represent a past event, or plan a future one, we are using the iconic mode. Drawing is an obvious example. A drawing or painting has a close (if imperfect) correlation with the thing it stands for.

Mode 3. **Symbolic representation**. Symbols are arbitrary but powerful ways of representing ideas and abstractions. The word 'flower' bears no relation to the object but the way in which words can be combined and manipulated gives a flexible means of cognitive control and interaction. Logical and mathematical notation, such as numbers, are other examples of the symbolic mode.

Bruner pointed out that although the prevailing mode of representation will change with age — so that, for example, enactive forms are increasingly replaced by iconic forms — all three types of representation continue to be used throughout life. This is unlike Piaget's stages which are seen as reconstructions of earlier forms.

---

1. Riding a bicycle.
2. Designing a building.
3. Telling a joke.
4. Solving an algebraic equation.
5. Playing chess.
6. Describing a film you have seen.
7. Decorating a room.

Which of Bruner's modes of representation is used for each activity? How many involve more than one mode?

Perception, language, instruction and evolution

Bruner follows Piaget in seeing all knowledge as a form of construction, with the knower playing an active part. In addition, Bruner incorporated notions from information processing theory into his system. For instance, he stresses the close relationship between perception and cognition. Perception is seen as a decision-making process in which the perceiver has to decide what he or she is seeing. This decision is based on certain cues gained from the object being perceived, which are ordered in accordance with the schemes the perceiver has previously developed. On the basis of these cues, the observer 'guesses' or infers the nature of the object.

This active, mental effort to produce meaning is based on notions like intentionality and hypothesis-testing, and is seen as an intrinsic part of the cognitive architecture. Nevertheless, without the assistance of concerned helpers such as parents and teachers, progress will be limited. Bruner invented the term **scaffolding** to describe the way in which parents support the acquisition of language. And, like Vygotsky, he believed that cognitive development is essentially a shared activity: without instruction the child's spontaneous activities could not be transformed into rational thought. And he was interested in the process of tutoring.

In one study, similar to that of Wertsch *et al.* described earlier, mothers were asked to help their preschool age children to construct a model pyramid and were provided with both a completed model and the pieces to make a replica. An important insight was the way in which successful mothers paced their contributions depending on the learners' responses. Effective tutors, as you might expect, are those who monitor the receptivity of their students, intervening only when necessary and building on accumulated skills and knowledge.

Finally, Bruner drew our attention to the importance of evolutionary factors in understanding cognitive development, a distinction he shares with Vygotsky. The prolonged period of childhood and the associated importance of play is discussed in one of Bruner's most famous articles, 'The nature and uses of immaturity' (Bruner, 1972). In this he argues that it is not just the opportunities for learning that prolonged childhood offers that are important, but also the nature of those opportunities. To become properly assimilated into something as complex as human civilization requires education.

What is meant by 'scaffolding'?

FIGURE 16: Playing with sand is not only enjoyable but provides opportunities for experimentation and gaining knowledge

SOMETHING TO TRY

Draw up a matrix with the names of Piaget, Vygotsky and Bruner along the top and typical components of theories of cognitive development down the side. Try to fill in the resulting boxes with a brief description of the place each feature holds (if any) in their theory. Examples of components to go down the left hand side of your matrix: LANGUAGE, ACTION, STAGES, SOCIAL INTERACTION, CULTURE, MENTAL STRATEGIES, INNATE FACTORS, MATURATION.

Piaget, Vygotsky and Bruner: Comparisons and contrasts

1. All three theorists — Piaget, Vygotksy and Bruner — emphasize the necessity of a developmental approach for understanding thought and language.

2. All three give a central role to the active, rather than reactive, child. For Piaget, action is an individually-based constructivist notion, whereas Vygotsky and Bruner talk more of activity as a social phenomenon.

3. For all three, cognitive development is seen as an adaptive process, having its roots in a biological process in common with other animals. With Vygotsky and Bruner the emphasis changes as the child gets older — see below.

4. In his response to Vygotsky's criticism of his account of egocentric speech, Piaget agreed with Vygotsky that the early function of language must be global communication and that later speech becomes differentiated into egocentric and communicative speech proper.

5. All three theorists place great importance on the study of scientific concepts in the child. Bruner, in particular, seeks to include a theory of instruction within this programme of study.

6. All chart development as taking place on roughly the same time scale with true concepts (or operations) not appearing until early adolescence. Piaget's system is much the most elaborate and Vygotsky's the least.

7. There are many similarities in methodological approach, such as careful observation of natural behaviour to try to discover underlying thought processes.

8. Piaget does not accept the directive (regulative) role of language in thinking central to much Soviet psychology.

9. Piaget suggests that language is only one, albeit important, dimension of representation. Vygotsky does not restrict thinking to language, but he has relatively little to say about nonverbal thinking. Bruner provides a theory of representation of relevance over the whole life-span.

10. Instruction is an important feature of Vygotsky's theory together with the idea of co-operative learning through the zone of proximal development. Bruner is broadly in agreement with this approach. In some contrast, self-action and learning by discovery is Piaget's key to the acquisition of knowledge.

11. In their explanations of mental growth, all three theorists refer to internalization. For Piaget, the internalization of actions makes mental problems reversible and allows the development of organized, relatively stable structures. For Vygotsky, the role of speech is central as the mediating tool by which cultures transmit ideas and by which these ideas become internalized. Bruner also stresses the role of language and offers a more sophisticated account of the role of social interaction.

Information Processing Theory

Psychologists who have adopted the metaphor of the human mind as an information processor with limited capacity, like the computer, are legion. Some have focused their attention on cognitive development. Frequently they have used the ideas of Piaget (e.g. Robert Case) or, less often, Vygotsky (e.g. Ann Brown) and they supplement these with notions derived from information processing theory. So, in this sense, there is no pure information processing theory of cognitive development. What the approach offers, however, is 'a more exact specification of what information is relevant to performance on a particular task and on how information is stored and manipulated by the child' (McShane, 1991, p.10).

Processing capacity and memory

(You may find it helpful to read the companion Unit Remembering and Forgetting by Annette Cassells in relation to what follows.)

It has long been known that an adult's short-term memory is limited to about seven items (Miller, 1956), for example the average telephone number. It turns out that this is a developmental phenomenon, and that the digit span — the number of digits a child hears and can repeat — increases with age. It starts at about 2—3 items at age two, but does not reach the adult level until adolescence (see Figure 17). While it is plain that older children show greater capacity to process information than younger children, what is not clear is how maturational factors (such as brain growth) together with relevant experience combine to account for this development.

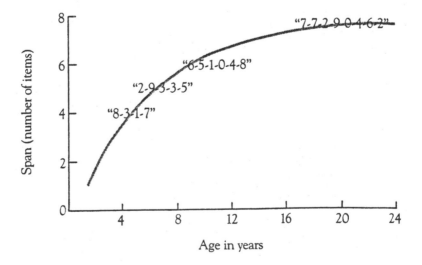

FIGURE 17: The number of digits that can be repeated accurately goes up steadily with age — one measure of memory span. (From *Human Development* by Fischer and Lazerson. Copyright © 1984 by Kurt W. Fischer and Arlyne Lazerson. Used with permission of W. H. Freeman and Company.)

Processing strategies and memory

Ways of handling information effectively also change with age. To take the example of memory: a basic strategy used by adults for remembering things is rehearsal — repeating things over and over to oneself. Research indicates that rehearsal is not used by five-year-olds at all and is not used reliably until nine to ten years. If five-year-olds are told to rehearse in order to help them remember something they will do so and improve, but on retesting they will fail to use this strategy spontaneously (Keeney, *et al*, 1967). It has also been found that when learning a list of words, eight-year-olds will typically repeat each individual word, while at 13 years they will practise them in groups. The older children are effectively adopting two strategies, rehearsal and *organization*.

Organization is most obvious when people are given lists of words involving a number of categories and asked to recall them in any order they like. Typically, they remember more words in free recall than in serial order recall because they can cluster the words into categories and report, say, all the animal words, then all the colours, clothes and so on. This technique might be used in something like Kim's Game, the children's party game where twenty or so familiar objects are placed on a tray. After some minutes of studying the objects, the tray is covered with a cloth. The winner is the one who remembers most items. Organization of information is a strategy that improves through the school years and can be taught but only older children use it spontaneously.

Two other common memory strategies are *elaboration* and *systematic searching*. Elaboration is similar to organization and involves finding a shared meaning or common element in the things to be remembered. In music, the mnemonic for remembering notes on the treble stave — Every Good Boy Deserves Favours — is one example. Not everyone is equally good at this, and conscious elaboration is a late developing skill.

SOMETHING TO TRY

Think of examples of how you have used organizational (including elaboration) strategies and how they have assisted you in, for example, studying for exams.

Processing strategies and recall

The strategies discussed so far are **storage** mechanisms. The other half of the memory equation involves retrieving what has been stored. Although effective storage strategies almost invariably aid remembering, we also use other strategies specifically for **retrieval**. One example is the *search* strategy. Keniston and Flavell (1979) asked participants aged between 6 and 18 to write down, on individual cards, letters of the alphabet that were read out to them. Then they were given a surprise memory test. It was found that those participants who used a search strategy — going through the alphabet systematically and deciding if that letter had been present — did much better. It was easy to detect such people because they recalled the letters, which had been presented randomly, in alphabetical order. Like many other cognitive skills, the efficient use of retrieval strategies is a late-developing ability.

Rule-based strategies: Robert Siegler

An example of an information processing approach to higher level cognitive activity, like problem solving, is the work of Robert Siegler. Building on Piaget's work, Siegler (1978) argues that much of cognitive development can be seen as the acquisition of general rules which can be applied to a range of problems. These rules develop in a particular sequence — remember, Piaget also made this point — and become increasingly powerful. Using tasks based on Piaget's experiments, Siegler demonstrated four rules that could account for the performance of children from 5 to 17 years. His best known study used a balance scale with pegs at regular intervals on to which weights (of a single value) could be hung (Figure 18).

Figure 18: The type of scale used by Seigler in his investigation of rule-based strategies

After the weights were distributed, children were asked to say which way the balance would fall when the lever holding it in position was released. The findings were as follows:

Rule 1. Initially, the child takes into account only one dimension, the number of weights; the greater number of weights is always judged to be the heavier, regardless of their value. This amounts to a *preoperational rule* in Piaget's terms.

Rule 2. Later on, judgements are still made on the basis of number of weights except when there are the same number on each side. In this case distance from the centre which, of course, may be a critical variable, is taken into account. This is a *transitional rule*.

Rule 3. Next, an attempt is made to take both distance and weight into account simultaneously, but if there is a conflict, for example, if one side has more weights but they are closer to the mid-point, the child will guess. This may be likened to a *concrete-operational rule* in Piaget's terms.

Rule 4. Finally, the child is now able to use a formula (distance x total actual weight for each side) to determine which way the balance will fall. This is equivalent to Piaget's *formal operational rule*.

Using empirical tasks like this, Siegler concluded that before the age of five, scientific reasoning in children is not rule governed. After that they develop an increasingly sophisticated rule-governed approach following the order of rules 1—4. When encountering new problems, children will tend to resort to lower level, general, all-purpose rules — what Siegler calls 'fall-back rules'. With experience the competence of the solution increases, often through an ability to take account of more than one dimension of the problem at a time.

The information processing approach: summary and conclusion

☐ Whether or not there is an increase in the basic processing capacity of the cognitive system with age remains debatable. One view is that capacity does increase as shown, for example, in the increase in digit span. An alternative view is that capacity is constant but the ability to make effective use of it — by **information handling techniques** — develops.

☐ Knowledge about any given task increases with a child's increasing experience, exploration and instruction. This leads to more efficient ways of remembering and solving problems.

☐ There is evidence for new strategies being acquired in a particular order. A relatively late accomplishment is the ability to monitor one's actions and demonstrate knowledge about one's own cognitive capacities, known as the metacognitive function. (We will come back to this.)

☐ With development, there comes the ability to apply existing strategies to more and more domains with ever increasing flexibility. In addition, a wider range of strategies can be applied to the *same* problem. This means that if the first proposed solution doesn't work an alternative can be tried.

☐ The information processing approach has been useful in moving beyond Piaget's somewhat global notion of structure to a more detailed account of the basic processes that change with age such as **encoding**, decoding, remembering, planning and analysing.

☐ Advances in our understanding of information processing, with its task analysis approach, allow us to make more effective interventions in the area of cognitive disorders, particularly education (see Part 8)

☐ Information processing approaches provide a number of models rather than a general theory in the sense of Piaget or Vygotsky. The scope is rather narrow, and there is little concern with a wider view of human development including its sociocultural, biological and evolutionary aspects.

Some Issues in Cognitive Development

KEY AIMS: By the end of Part 6 you will have some understanding of:
▷   whether what we think about (people or things) requires different types of cognition
▷   the significance of context in thinking
▷   the role of metacognition — knowing what you know
▷   what is meant by a theory of mind
▷   the significance of the false belief task.

Thinking about objects and thinking about people

It seems unlikely that we have two different types of cognition, one for dealing with people and one for use with the world of objects. After all, the head that deals with the physical world is the same as that which interacts with the social world. Nevertheless, it is unwise to dismiss out of hand the idea of separate social and nonsocial cognitions. For instance, it has been shown that performance in certain tasks, such as object permanence, seems more advanced when the object is a person — see the companion Unit on *Perception* by Cassells and Green for a discussion of **object permanence**. It is also the case that Piaget's theory of cognitive development was based almost entirely on the child's engagement with the physical world. Since there are important differences between the animate and inanimate world (summarized in Table 1), there are, at the very least, grounds for looking at this more closely.

	Animate	Inanimate
INHERENT PROPERTIES	change, grow, reproduce	need external agent
	entities that think, feel & socialize	'Inert'
	complex biological structure	possibly complex but not entities
AS OBJECTS OF PERCEPTION	physical properties + actions, intentions motives, feelings	physical properties only
	reciprocity — 2-way communication	do not perceive us
AS RECIPIENTS OF ACTION	not always predictable	predictable
	agents to act on inanimate or animate	instruments not agents
	pursue goals	not goal orientated
KNOWLEDGE	psychological principles	physical laws

TABLE 1: A comparison of the animate and inanimate world: implications for social cognitive theorizing (After Gelman and Spelke (1981))

The principal difference between people and objects is that people are reactive, **reciprocal** beings that are not merely acted upon. You can stroke, strike, verbally abuse, and even try to feed a block of wood but you won't get much reaction. Do any of these things to a human being and you cannot safely predict the outcome! Thus far the empirical evidence suggests that theories grounded in the physical world do have relevance to social affairs, for example, in the area of moral development (Damon, 1977), but an adequate theory of cognition needs to take social knowledge into account, and we will return to this later.

The role of context

Distinguishing thinking about persons from thinking about objects is one example of how context is important. But context is broader than this. All human cognitive activity takes place in a context even if you are only sitting in a chair thinking. Do you think more effectively in a quiet room or when music is playing in the background? Are problems easier to solve when working alone or with others? Such questions, of course, can be explored empirically.

Let us take the example that children work better at a conservation task in pairs than alone. Piaget's explanation would be that the children offer alternative judgements and this leads to cognitive conflict (equilibration) which is a necessary step to the development of a new cognitive structure. Vygotsky's interpretation would emphasize the role of negotiation and the zone of proximal development to account for the same result.

Another dimension of context is discussed by Donaldson (1978). It is taken as self-evident that children are always trying to make sense of their world but that, in doing so, they find that some situations and some interpretations are more acceptable than others. It is quite possible that children, in trying to make sense of the world, will look to adults for cues. In the conservation experiment, for example, where an adult takes a large ball of plasticine and changes it into three smaller balls, 'human sense', as Donaldson called it, might suggest to the child that there is now likely to be *more* plasticine.

So, what happens if we test the child using situations that they have more direct experience of? When this was done using an adaptation of the three mountains experiment — the new problem was to judge where someone could hide in a street to escape a policeman — children were found to do much better and to show much less egocentrism.

What do you think Donaldson means by the term 'human sense'? How might it influence our interpretation of children's performance on Piagetian tasks?

Context is also about **domains**. We know that individuals are not equally competent in all aspects of their cognitive lives. Some may be better at French than at mathematics; others better at science than at history. So, it may be unsafe to assume that a particular level of cognitive development is the same in tasks which make different sorts of demands. A child may do well with numbers but poorly with spatial reasoning. There is now more caution about accepting global theories of cognitive development in preference to what has been called **situated cognition** (Light and Butterworth, 1992).

In science it is generally preferable to construct theories that have a broad usage and can be applied to the widest range of circumstances. However, the field of cognitive development has, in recent years, seen the proliferation of more modest theoretical accounts that aid understanding and practical intervention in specific areas like reading and mathematics. Ultimately we probably need both types of account.

Metacognitive growth — knowing what we know

The development of knowledge is not the whole cognitive story: if we want to regulate and control our mental skills we also need to know what we know. This is called **metacognition**. There are two main aspects.

1. The development of understanding and knowledge of one's own cognitive capacity — knowing, for instance, that you will not remember someone's telephone number unless you write it down.

2. The development of the ability to regulate one's mental world. This is the idea of an **executive** function that monitors and controls ongoing cognitive performance and, in so doing, is able to detect problems in either output or input and react accordingly. Let me explain.

Research has shown that children's knowledge of their own cognitive capabilities begins to develop in the school years. The more aware children are, for instance, of the sorts of mnemonic strategies that were discussed earlier, the less time they will spend using inefficient procedures — they are learning how to learn. Similarly, to know how to evaluate information, say a set of verbal instructions, underpins success in many educational and work situations.

Markman (1979) showed how children in the early school years are slow to realize they have not understood something. In one task primary school children were given deliberately inadequate instructions on how to play a card game. Seven-year-olds failed to realize they had insufficient information to play the game even after a number of probing questions. It was only when they actually played the game that they understood the problem. Eleven-year-olds were able to monitor their comprehension much more effectively and to detect the inadequacy of the instructions.

Metacognition is very important for effective learning and is unusual in being one of the areas of cognitive development that develops most noticeably during and after adolescence. Indeed, it can be argued that a lot of what differentiates the very successful from the average student (at any age) is the degree to which the person is aware of what they can do, and the extent to which they monitor performance and distribute effort on the basis of this knowledge.

A POSSIBLE PROJECT

Construct a piece of text or a set of instructions which contains ambiguities, contradictions and omissions. Try this out with your fellow students, or younger students (11—12 years). You may present the material orally or in written form. (Does it make a difference?) Ask your participants if they understand what they have read or what you have told them. In the written version you could get them to underline any passages they find problematic. What sorts of things get noticed and what sorts of things get missed? How do younger people differ from older ones? What does this tell you about metacognitive processes?

The child's theory of mind

The child's growing understanding of the mind is metacognition with a significant social component. We cannot predict and explain the behaviour of others if we do not know how to gauge their mental states.

The main way of investigating this is by using what is known as the **false belief** task (Wimmer and Perner, 1983). False belief, in this sense, doesn't refer to outright lying but to the child's ability to ascribe to another person a belief that is different from their own. This demonstrates possession of a theory of mind. Theory of mind is a complex notion but, put simply, it refers to the realization that another's state of mind may, or may not, be the same as yours. Although the comparison is not exact, you could say that to lack a theory of mind is the same as acting egocentrically, that is, assuming everyone sees the world in the same way as you.

The standard false belief task takes the form of a story or it can be acted out — see Figure 19

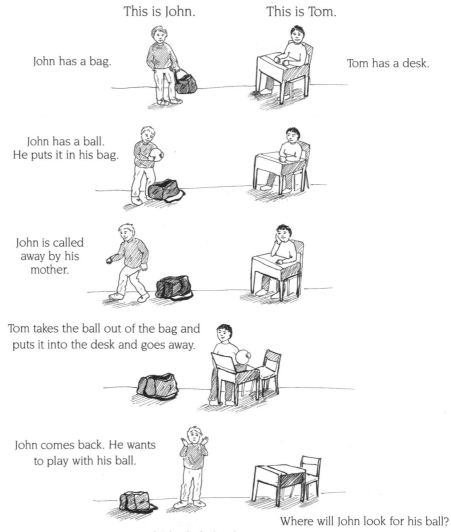

FIGURE 19: Example of a typical false belief task

For instance, the child is told that Jane's mother puts a bar of chocolate in a drawer while Jane is watching. Jane leaves the room and while she is away the chocolate is taken from the drawer and put into a cupboard. The child is asked where he or she thinks Jane will look for the chocolate when she comes back. Most three-year-olds predict that Jane will look in the cupboard, where the chocolate actually is. They credit Jane with their own correct belief. Most five-year-olds realize that Jane will act on the basis of what she knows (now a false belief): that the chocolate is in the drawer. Four-year-olds are in a transitional phase. They will tend to respond like three-year-olds but if they are prompted — 'Where did Jane see her mother put the chocolate?'; 'Where did her mother put it next?' — they are able to make the correct judgement.

Three-year-olds are also bad at recognizing their *own* false beliefs. When presented with a familiar Smartie box which, on examination, contains not Smarties but pencils, they say that their friend will think that there are pencils in the box. When asked what they thought was in the box originally, they reply 'Pencils'! (Perner *et al.* 1987).

It looks, therefore, as if an important breakthrough in understanding the mental states of others is made between three and five years; one that throws new light on the concept of egocentrism and which influences social transactions between pre-school children. It is possible that childhood **autism** can be explained, at least partly, by the failure to develop an adequate theory of mind (Baron-Cohen *et al.*, 1985).

What is meant by theory of mind? What can five-year-olds understand that three-year-olds cannot?

7 Language Development

KEY AIMS: By the end of Part 7 you should:
> understand some of the historical accounts of language development
> be familiar with the main stages of language development
> understand the significance of the prelinguistic phase
> know the course of vocabulary growth and the role of social routines
> understand some of the important factors in language acquisition including the role of learning, information processing and the nature/nurture issue.
> have some understanding of the development of word meanings and grammar.
> be familiar with some issues to do with language impairment and the role of critical periods.

Theories of cognitive development often omit language development but since speaking and listening are obviously part of cognition we will not do so. You will discover that some of the issues that surround the acquisition of language lie outside those that concern theories of cognitive development. But other issues, such as the nature/nurture debate, are also relevant to language growth.

Language is not a single entity but a complex group of systems consisting of sounds (**phonology**), meaning (**semantics**), grammar (**syntax**) and contextual features (**pragmatics**). The remarkable fact is that children acquire all these things in a very short space of time; most are competent users of language by the time they start school. This linguistic ability seems to be unique — children have no comparable ability in the area of numbers or reading. It appears that we have an inbuilt capacity for acquiring what is a specifically human characteristic.

(If you have not already done so, it would be useful at this point to read Part 1 of the companion Unit, Language and Thought by Judith Hartland, which describes the components of language.)

A brief history

The serious study of language development and the discipline of **psycho-linguistics** began as recently as the 1960s with the revolutionary impact of Noam Chomsky. Chomsky's account refers to a deep mental structure forming the basis of the language system and from which surface forms — what we actually say and hear — are derived using **transformational rules**. These are procedures by which a base form, such as 'Mary strokes the dog', can be converted into other propositions like 'Did Mary stroke the dog?' and 'The dog was stroked by Mary'. The hypothesizing of such built-in rules is thought to be an economical explanation for what happens, and reflects a strong nativist bias in Chomsky's theory.

This was taken up by psychologists who were impressed by the speed with which children learn to speak. How else could such a complex system be acquired so quickly unless there is a built-in capacity? In support of this was biological evidence showing that language milestones (first word, two words, short sentence, and so on) correlate much more highly with maturationally-determined motor milestones (crawling, walking, standing on one leg) than with age (Lenneberg, 1969) (Table 2)

Age (years)	Motor milestones	Language milestones
0.5	Sits using hands for support; unilateral standing.	Cooing sounds change to babbling by introduction of consonantal sounds.
1	Stands; walks when held by one hand.	Syllabic reduplication; signs of understanding some words, applies some sounds regularly to signify persons or objects, that is, the first words.
1.5	Prehension and release fully developed; gait propulsive; creeps downstairs backwards.	Repertoire of 3 to 50 words not joined in phrases; trains of sounds and intonation patterns resembling discourse; good progress in understanding.
2	Runs (with falls); walks down stairs with one foot forward only.	More than 50 words; two-word phases most common; more interest in verbal communication; no babbling.
2.5	Jumps with both feet; stands on one foot for 1 second; builds tower of six cubes.	Each day new words; utterances of three or more words; seems to understand almost everything said to him; still many grammatical deviations.
3	Tiptoes 3 yards (2.7 metres); walks stairs with alternating feet; jumps 0.9 metre.	Vocabulary of some 1000 words; about 80% intelligibility; grammar of utterances close approximation to colloquial adult; syntactic mistakes fewer in variety, systematic, predictable.
4.5	Jumps over rope; hops on one foot; walks on line.	Language well established; grammatical anomalies restricted either to unusual constructions or to the more literate aspects of discourse.

(Reprinted with permission from E.H. Lennenberg. On explaining language. *Science*, 164, 1969) Copyright 1969 American Association for the Advancement of Science.

TABLE 2: The relationship between motor and language development is quite close

Almost as important as Chomsky's theoretical ideas was the methodology used by linguists which caused psychologists to revise their approach. When linguists study an unfamiliar language they collect as large a sample of the language (a corpus) as they can, and attempt to write a grammar to fit it. They are helped, of course, by existing grammars, possibly in related languages, and by the insights of native speakers. It occurred to the early developmental psycholinguists, such as Martin Braine and Roger Brown, that it would be helpful to treat child language in the same way, as an exotic form of communication. So, they set out to collect samples of child speech and to write child grammars in order to specify the rules underlying children's utterances.

By the early 1970s it was apparent that an account of language development that relied on the grammatical structure of the utterance was insufficient. Children seemed to be expressing more in their speech output than was shown by the linguistic form alone. To know whether the utterance 'Jane drink' was a declarative statement — 'This is Jane's drink' — or a request — 'May I have a drink?' — the context of the utterance was vital. The so-called method of '**rich interpretation**' (Bloom, 1970) showed a whole range of different semantic relations and meanings of two-word sentences once the *preceding words* as well as the *nonverbal context* were considered.

Once context was added to accounts of language development the way was open for social and interpersonal factors to enter the picture (Bates, 1976; Bruner, 1976). This provided a valuable counterweight to the earlier nativist and cognitive theories. The sociolinguist Hymes made the distinction between linguistic and communicative competence. Linguistic competence is the knowledge of the syntactic and semantic rules of language. In English, for example, there is a grammatical rule for negating a statement that usually involves putting 'not' in front of the verb. Communicative competence is the ability to use language appropriately in real, everyday situations. Very often it is important to get your message across clearly and with impact, such as when you are being interviewed. (Another example is to imagine that you are writing copy for an advertisement for jeans. Which is more important, grammar or communicative strength?)

The significance of this distinction depends on our focus of interest. Are we interested in what people know about language (linguistic competence) or in what they can do with it (communicative competence)? And how is the business of making ourselves understood achieved? This takes the rich interpretation approach a step further. If you want to know how communication succeeds or fails you need to look at conversations between children *and their caretakers* and, in so doing, to consider the role of input and of individual differences.

Seeing language as the growth of *communication* opened the way for a more clearly psychological (rather than purely linguistic) contribution to the area. An increasing interest in how meaning was assimilated was also of central concern to psychologists given the intimate link between semantics and conceptual categories.

Currently the area of language acquisition is a lively, and contentious, field of enquiry; there is little agreement about even fundamental issues such as the role of the verbal input that the child hears. This presents problems for a brief and introductory exposition, but my aim is to describe the course of language development, what is acquired, and how it is to be explained.

Describe two main influences on the study of language development since the 1960s.

Stages in acquiring language

The pre-linguistic phase

There is good evidence that, from the beginning, infants are able to discriminate between different sounds which correspond to the basic segments of the language known as **phonemes**. Initially, this ability is not confined to their mother tongue. Within a year, however, infants learn which sounds are relevant to their own language and lose the ability to discriminate phoneme differences for other languages (Eimas, 1985).

Infants are less precocious in producing sounds, and **babbling** — early sound play producing noises like 'bababa' and 'adadada' — doesn't begin until the second half of the first year. This limited repertoire doesn't prevent parents indulging in conversations with their offspring:

Child: (smiles)
Mother: Oh what a nice little smile. Yes isn't that nice? There. There's a nice little smile.
Child: (burps)
Mother: What a nice little wind as well. Yes, that's better isn't it? Yes. Yes.
Child: (vocalizes)
Mother: There's a nice noise.

(Snow, 1977)

What is happening in such 'conversations'? Adults seem to treat babies as though they were co-operative partners in a conversation, even though in reality the mother is, as one psychologist puts it, 'holding up both ends of the dialogue'. Some theorists argue that through such a process infants learn what it is to be a participant in a social event like conversation (Trevarthen, 1978). In this way they become, in due course, reciprocating and truly social people.

Perhaps the most important point about the pre-linguistic phase is that even if language is not yet evident, the infant is acquiring a great deal of other knowledge. The world has 'meaning' for the infant before the advent of language; words can then map on to these existing sensorimotor schemes.

The growth of vocabulary

Words proper start to appear at around 12 months and given what has been said about already available knowledge, it is unsurprising that the early **lexicon** reflects the objects and events in the baby's life. Talk is about people, animals, toys, food, body parts, household articles and so on.

The appearance of the first word does not signal an immediate spurt in vocabulary growth. Indeed, to start with progress is slow, with the first 10 words taking an additional three to four months (Nelson, 1973). New words are added every few days up to the 50-word point when, at around 18 months, there is a sudden burst of growth in vocabulary which may multiply 5- or 10-fold in only a few weeks. This usually coincides with the onset of word combinations (Figure 20). An impressive rate of new word acquisition follows throughout the pre-school period. From a vocabulary at 18 months of, say, 25 words, the child moves to about 15000 words at six years; an average of nine new words a day.

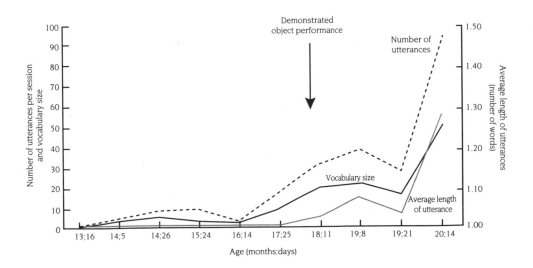

Figure 20: This illustration of one child's language growth shows that relatively little happens before 16 months then both number of utterances and vocabulary size increase. Soon after the reliable demonstration of object permanance is achieved, all measures rise sharply. (From *Human Development* by Fischer and Lazerson. Copyright © 1984 by Kurt W Fischer and Arlyne Lazerson. Used with permisson of W.H. Freeman and Company.)

What can account for this impressive feat? This sort of expansion can't depend on the child being carefully taught each new word. Children seem to manage this by themselves, adding new words and phrases to their repertoire as they meet them in daily conversation. In doing this they use context to give meaning and make use of their available knowledge. Nevertheless, in the earliest stages there is also evidence for a 'teaching' component. Ninio and Bruner (1978) emphasize the role of regular, daily routines (which Bruner calls **formats**) between toddlers and their parents, which enable the child to gain understanding about social relationships and other knowledge. Language is special in being at the same time a social and a cognitive enterprise. Take 'book reading', when parent and small child sit side by side looking at a picture book. The sort of dialogue that takes place is as follows:

Mother: Look! (ATTENTIONAL VOCATIVE)
Child: (Touches picture)
M: What are those? (QUERY)
C: (Vocalizes and smiles)
M: Yes, they are rabbits. (FEEDBACK & LABEL)
C: (Vocalizes, smiles and looks up at mother)
M: (Laughs) Yes, rabbit. (FEEDBACK & LABEL)
C: (Vocalizes, smiles)
M: Yes (laughs) (FEEDBACK)

Figure 21: At this age, looking at a book together is not about learning to read but is a useful way of enlarging the child's repertoire of object names.

The significance of the book reading format is that it focuses the child's attention on particular, shared objects and events, allowing the adult to provide the appropriate name with the necessary encouragement and feedback. It is, according to Bruner, an important part of the process by which children learn that specific words refer to specific objects, actions and more complex concepts.

SAQ
17

How might we account for the growth spurt in vocabulary?

Words and meanings

Observational studies of semantic development have demonstrated a phenomenon called **overextension**, where a word is used in relation to events or objects beyond those which the word would normally be used for. Anyone talking to a two-year-old will quickly discover this. Thus a child may use the word 'doggy' to refer to other furry, four-legged creatures of a certain size with a tail. Whether the child does this because he or she believes that sheep *are* dogs, or simply because he hasn't another word to represent the distinction, is a difficult question to answer. What is clear is that the growth of word meaning is often idiosyncratic and that one child's semantic field for 'ball' or 'cat' may overlap only slightly with another's.

For example, my eldest child's semantic field for vehicles or transport developed over a period of about six months beginning with an onomatopoeic term derived from aircraft (Table 3). Many mothers have been embarrassed by their two-year-old approaching a strange man and calling him 'Daddy'! It is only later that the child understands that this label is only appropriate for one particular adult male.

TABLE 3: One child's developing semantic field: 'transport'

'woo'	=	aeroplane
'by'	=	motor bike
		own wooden toy three-wheeler
		pedal cycle
		own toy tractor
		push chair
'da'	=	car (+ lorry, bus, tractor, etc)
'lo-lo'	=	lorry
		bus
		tractor
		large vehicles
'bu'	=	bus
'ca-ca'	=	tractor

Qualifiers. Experimental studies of word meaning tend to focus on classes of words that perform important functions in language but whose meaning is not usually concrete, as it is for most nouns. Examples are prepositions, dimensional adjectives (tall/short; wide/narrow) and quantifiers (all/none; more/less). Here it is found that initially the meaning is fuzzy and children rely more strongly on nonlinguistic properties of the context in which the word is used rather than the dictionary meaning. Clark (1973) found, for example, that when children were asked to place a small object, such as a toy animal, in, on, or under a larger object (Figure 22), two-year-olds were profoundly affected by context.

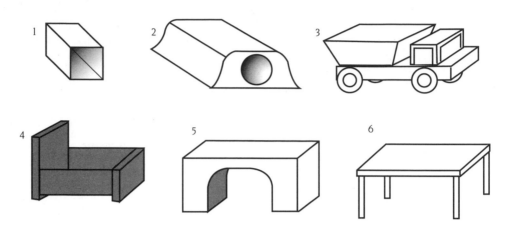

FIGURE 22: Material used by Eve Clark to investigate children's understanding of spatial prepositions. (From Clark, E. (1973). *Cognition* 2 (2). Elsevier Science.)

If the instruction was 'Put the cat *on* the table', they would do so but if asked to put the cat *under* the table, they would still put it on the table. Similarly they would put objects *in* but not *on* a box. Even more telling was that when only required to imitate an action, such as putting an object *beside* the box, most two-year-olds would put it *in* the box.

This is powerful evidence that young children use their existing knowledge to interpret language. Boxes are usually containers; tables usually act as supporting surfaces. If you want to know if a child understands the preposition 'on' it is better to ask him or her to put the saucer on the cup rather than the expected standard relationship, cup on saucer.

Quantifiers. Quantifiers, such as all/none, more/less, are similarly confused. Thus, preschool children asked to judge which of two glasses had more juice responded correctly. But they made the same choice when asked to select the glass that had less juice (Donaldson, 1978). It might be that they simply prefer larger quantities, of course.

It also reflects the important point that relational pairs of words, like 'more' and 'less' and 'same' and 'different', do not have a straightforward meaning. Indeed, an object (a ball) might be the same as another object (another ball) and, at the same time, different from it (a larger ball). As Donaldson has argued, one of the reasons that children might have difficulty with Piaget's tasks like conservation and classification is because of the language used in the experimental instructions.

In what ways does children's use of words differ from adults'?

Development of grammar

At the two-word stage it is possible to talk of a grammar of child language. Here we are talking of speech like 'more book', 'no wash' and 'look doggy'. As well as being short, these early utterances lack grammatical **markers** or **inflections** such as '-s' for plural and '-ed' for past tense. Also omitted are some of the function words like articles ('a', 'the') and auxiliaries ('be', 'do'). Children's early sentences — and not just in English — seem to have common forms. Their utterances reflect the here and now, and ignore past and future. They consist of words that are stressed in normal usage — nouns, verbs and adjectives — which are the cues that an information processing account would predict. In turn, this leads to a telegraphic style of speech in which 'drop cup' is used to stand for 'I have dropped my cup'.

Although talk of a 'grammar' at the two-word stage may seem exaggerated, it is possible to write grammatical rules for early child language. Braine (1963) divided the components of early sentences into two classes: the *pivot* and the *open*. The examples given in the previous paragraph, such as 'more book', are typical of pivot — open constructions. The word 'more' is used to qualify many other words (usually nouns) that would fit into the second slot — 'book', and 'TV'. So the pivot corresponds roughly to a modifying category consisting of adjectives, verbs and quantifiers, while the open class is typically nouns. Brown (1973) later showed that it is possible to go beyond this dichotomy to differentiate a much larger variety of forms (see Table 4).

TABLE 4: The first sentences in child speech

Structural meaning	Form	Example
1. Nomination	that+N	that book
2. Notice	hi+N	hi belt
3. Recurrence	more+N	
	'nother+N	more milk
4. Nonexistence	allgone+N	
	no more+N	allgone rattle
5. Attributive	Adj+N	big train
6. Possessive	N+N	mommy lunch
7. Locative	N+N	Sweater chair
8. Locative	V+N	walk street
9. Action-agent	N+V	Eve read
10. Agent-object	N+N	Mommy sock
11. Action-object	V+N	put book
12. Conjunction	N+N	umbrella boot

(Adapted from R. Brown, *Psycholinguistics*. New York: Free Press, 1970. p.220.)

From the two-word stage children progress to more complex sentences including inflections as well as more words. Brown (1973) identified a developmental sequence where *-ing* was the earliest inflection followed by the prepositions *on* and *in*. Then came another inflection, the plural *-s* on nouns; irregular past tenses such as *broke* and *came*; possessives; articles; the *-s* that is added to third person verbs; the regular past tense *-ed*; and various forms of the auxiliary verb. Why the order is as it is remains a puzzle but again there appears to be a relationship with the amount of information processing required by each form.

Describe three things that distinguish children's grammar from adults'.

Explanations of language development

The role of learning

It is self-evident that learning plays a role in language development since we all speak our native language and, indeed, the accent we hear. It is a much stronger claim, however, to argue that processes like imitation and conditioning account for the course of language growth. Do children copy only what they hear? Clearly imitation plays a role in situations like Ninio and Bruner's book reading. But it can't be the sole means by which language is acquired, if only because all children frequently say things which they have never heard an adult say, such as 'allgone rattle'. And when asked to repeat adult utterances they produce their own telegraphic form. So, 'Half a pound of tuppenny rice" becomes 'half pound rice'. Also, the mistakes that children make in their speech — 'me breaked it' — suggest that an attempt is being made to apply their own rules rather than simply copy what they have heard.

It has also been suggested that children are conditioned or trained to learn language by being rewarded by parents for using correct forms. A conditioning explanation is also implausible. If children were rewarded for producing grammatical utterances and given negative **reinforcement** for errors, an enormous and detailed commitment on the part of parents would be required. The evidence is that parents overlook grammatical errors and attend to what the child appears to mean (Brown *et al.*, 1969).

Information processing

Earlier in this Unit we talked about the following of rules. There is good reason to believe that children abstract rules from the linguistic input they receive and apply them — a sort of hypothesis testing — when they speak. The most convincing evidence is the existence of errors when children overgeneralize, or misapply, the rule. A familiar example is to add 's' for the pluralization of irregular forms so that both 'mans' and 'mens' are common. Kuczaj (1977) showed that for the past tense of verbs the order of acquisition is:

1. Correct irregular form — 'broke'

2. Use of regular 'ed' forms — 'jumped'

3. Overregularization of the irregular — 'breaked'

4. Correct use of regular and irregular forms.

It seems there are a number of principles operating in learning to talk and understanding speech and these guide the generation of hypotheses. After analysing a large number of languages, Slobin (1973) compiled the following processing rules. The complexity of these rules demonstrates what a difficult business language learning is.

☐   Look for systematic changes in the form of words.

- ☐ Look for grammatical markers (such as, *not, -ed*) that clearly indicate changes in meaning.

- ☐ Avoid exceptions (for example, irregular plural forms: man/men; sheep/sheep. The point being that these are a poor guide to the *normal* rule.)

- ☐ Pay attention to the ends of words. (Ends of words carry high information content such as *tense* of verbs and *number* for nouns.)

- ☐ Pay attention to the order of words, prefixes, and suffixes.

- ☐ Avoid interruption or rearrangement of constituents (that is, sentence units). (From Atkinson *et al.*, 1993; after Slobin, 1973.)

Nature versus nurture in language development

Nature. The pendulum has swung back and forth in the debate about the respective influences of inherited and environmental factors in language acquisition. Chomsky put forward three reasons for an innate facility for language learning — popularly known as the **Language Acquisition Device** (LAD) (McNeill, 1970). These are:

▷ that infants attend to speech elements rather than other noises in the environment;

▷ that they master a complex system in a remarkably short period of time;

▷ that they become effective speakers despite an often far from perfect (ungrammatical) input from the people around them.

At least one of these claims is dubious since it has been shown that instead of providing a degraded speech environment for their child, parents plan their utterances and speak in a way that makes it easier to acquire both meaning and grammar. The most obvious example is the special **register** that adults use in talking to babies and small children, referred to as child-directed speech (see Box 4).

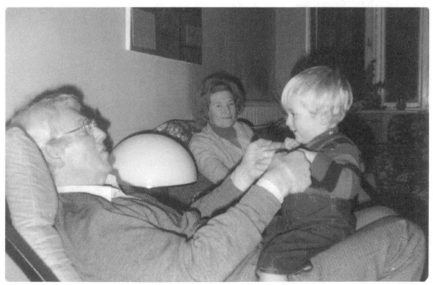

FIGURE 23: This is typical of the sort of face-to-face situations in which early learning communication takes place between adult and child.

BOX 4. Features of child-directed speech

1. It is spoken more slowly and at a higher pitch, with marked pauses at the end of sentences.

2. Short, grammatical sentences are used with few **modifiers** (such as adjectives) and **pro-forms** (such as pronouns).

3. Exaggerated stress patterns are used.

4. There is frequent use of repetition both of own speech and the child's utterances.

5. Repetitions are often accompanied by expansions or **recasts**. (Child: 'Daddy gone'. Mother: 'Yes Daddy's gone to the shops hasn't he?')

6. Familiar concrete vocabulary is used. The principle of most common usage is followed, so likely to say 'fish' rather than 'trout', 'cat' rather than 'animal'.

7. Use of endearments and nursery or diminuitive forms such as 'doggy', 'choo-choo', 'Mummy'.

8. Nonverbal features include exaggerated facial expressions and prolonged mutual gaze.

Some of these features are seen in the following short extract between a mother and her 18-month-old daughter.

Child: (blowing noises)
Mother: That's a bit rude.
C: Mouth.
M: Mouth, that's right.
C: Face.
M: Face, yes, mouth is in your face. What else have you got in your face?
C: Face (closing eyes).
M: You're making a face, aren't you?

The mother is using the child's contributions, however limited, to guide the conversation. Note the use of repetition and expansions of what the child has said which, it is assumed, act as a model for the child of how conversations can be extended.

The relationship between input and output

Nurture. An environmentalist account of language development would predict a close relationship between what children hear (the input) and what they say (the output). It is, in fact, not easy to demonstrate this (other than the obvious realization that we usually talk with the same accent as those around us). One finding is that parents who use a lot of repetitions or a lot of *wh-* questions (*who?* *what?*) have children who show more rapid grammatical development (Hoff-Ginsberg, 1986). Repetition helps by emphasizing the structure of language, and questions oblige the child to speak and maintain conversation.

There is some evidence that the frequent use of child-directed speech, especially expansions, does influence the pattern of language growth (Hirsh-Pasek, *et al.*, 1984). At the same time, all children acquire complex syntax, even if more slowly. This makes it difficult to claim that particular types of language input *cause* language development.

SOMETHING TO TRY

Next time you have the opportunity to observe an adult talking to a baby, note the characteristics of their language. How many of the features of child-directed speech listed above, figure in the behaviour? You might also catch yourself using some of these forms in talking to babies (before you become self-conscious!).

Critical periods

The idea that there are **critical periods** in human growth has long been established in other areas of developmental psychology. Applied to language it implies that if, for any reason, the child's access to language is severely limited in the early years and he or she hears very little, then their language development will be poor. There are, of course, very few instances of this — most children are not linguistically isolated. But occasionally it happens. Genie, a little girl in the USA, was confined to a small, bare room from the age of 20 months to 13 years when she was discovered. During this time she heard no speech and, when found, she understood no language. But her senses were normal and she did begin to learn to speak after being placed in a foster home.

Her language development followed the usual early stages — babbling, one word, two words, short sentences and so on — and she progressed as far as the level of a three-to four-year-old. But there were abnormal features: she never asked questions spontaneously and never learnt to use the '-ed' form for past tenses. She also had some problems with intonation — your experience of learning a foreign language might have taught you that to speak it without an accent it must be acquired in the early years (Curtiss, 1977).

So, what does the case of Genie tell us about a critical period in language development? Well, despite losing nearly 12 years, she did manage to acquire language. Clearly, however, her capacity was impaired and so the notion of a critical phase receives some but not absolute support.

Other evidence comes from studies of sign language used by deaf people. Surveys have found that those adults who were exposed to sign language from birth showed greater mastery of the syntax than those who learned at deaf school between four and six years. This group, in turn, was superior to those who did not learn to sign until after 12 years (Newport, 1990). This evidence for a critical period is particularly interesting given that all the sample had been using sign language for some 30 years — one would have thought that any early differences would have disappeared.

SAQ
20

What is meant by a critical period in language development and what evidence is there for it?

---

8 Applications

KEY AIMS

▷ To *acquaint you with the impact of Piaget in education and some of the issues raised by discovery learning.*

▷ To *examine the influence of Vygotsky and Bruner and the teacher's role as a transmitter of knowledge.*

▷ To *look at the role of language and literacy in cognitive development.*

▷ To *see how the information processing approach has uncovered processes involved in classroom learning.*

▷ To *look specifically at recent research in the child's understanding of mathematics.*

Although theories of cognitive development vary in the extent to which they aim to influence practical situations, all the theories we have discussed have had an applied impact. The most obvious area is education. So, what impact have these theories made on a particular skill like mathematics or learning to read? What has been the effect on classroom practice? Can we describe what is meant by 'normal intellectual development?' Can we specify what learning difficulties there might be?

The impact of Piaget's theory

In Britain, the influence of Piaget's theory, especially in the 5—11 year age group (primary school in the UK), has been considerable. The *Plowden Report* (1967), a major enquiry into the practice and nature of primary school teaching and learning in the UK, recommended that Piaget's theory should form the basis of teacher training; strong emphasis was now placed on child-centred, discovery learning. Teachers were taught to create opportunities for children to discover the principles that underlie events in the physical world.

Although he claimed not to be interested in education, Piaget did in fact write one book on this subject (Piaget, 1971). In that he states his position (quite clearly for Piaget!):

'If the child's thought is qualitatively different from our own, then the principal aim of education is to form its intellectual and moral reasoning power. Since that power cannot be formed from outside, the question is to find the most suitable methods and environment to help the child constitute it itself; in other words, to achieve coherence and objectivity on the intellectual plane and reciprocity on the moral plane.'

(Piaget, 1971: 160)

FIGURE 24: Even in the nursery school children can make important discoveries about the properties of things.

According to Piaget, teachers must recognize that children are, by nature, 'knowing' creatures. They are actively trying to construct their world, and teachers should avoid dulling their eagerness to discover by enforcing rigid curricula. It helps also to know what stage of intellectual development each child is at.

The idea that children are the principal architects of their own cognitive destinies appeals strongly to some teachers. Even more influential is the idea that the teaching of abstract knowledge must be preceded by a grounding in direct experience and concrete problem solving. Piaget mistrusted any approach which simply tried to cram facts into children. He called this low level learning, uninformed by understanding. Such approaches do not lead to the development of new cognitive structures. The information acquired is highly specific and devoid of the abstract concepts which enable the child to generalize a piece of knowledge. For example, mathematical functions like subtraction should be capable of generalization from one particular circumstance (shopping) to another, different one (playing cards).

But what teachers claim to believe doesn't always coincide with actual practice. Edwards and Mercer (1987) asked teachers what principles guided their teaching; they replied that they followed a broadly Piagetian philosophy. But when teachers were observed in lessons such as discovering the physical laws that governed the actions of a pendulum, it was seen that they provided a great many suggestions, hints and examples in their teaching. They behaved, in short, more like instructors, treating their students as apprentices — they were true Vygotskyans!

SAQ 21

What particular features of Piaget's theory are likely to be of interest to teachers?

Applications of Vygotsky's theory

The approaches of Vygotsky and of Bruner have a more obvious relevance to education. If cognitive growth is seen as dependent on the culture in which children are reared, then schools are clearly one of the most valuable parts of this cultural learning experience. Many teachers would welcome the notion that there is an important instructional element to knowledge and that learning should take account of every child's zone of proximal development. It seems obvious that children will do better on tasks, like reading or arithmetic, if they are given assistance. Nevertheless, part of the social constructivist approach is the belief that cognitive performance necessarily becomes an individual process. If the student is always reliant on the promptings of the instructor then the educational process can be said to have failed.

The role of language and literacy

Classroom communication

A key role is played by language in the classroom since it is used initially to regulate other people's behaviour and is then adopted by the student to regulate his or her own behaviour. Language is important, therefore, both to exchange ideas and as a means of organizing one's own ideas. The classroom is, above all, a verbal environment. It is one, moreover, that is dominated by the teacher. One of the major shifts that children must adapt to on entering full time education is the different communicative context. At home they talk about familiar topics, with familiar, supportive partners. At school they are one of many, talking (when they get the opportunity) often about strange issues with authority figures who, however friendly, cannot offer the one-to-one verbal support that parents do.

Besides, language in the classroom does not obey the familiar rules of dialogue. Instead, the child must deal with the flow of incoming messages, understand what is being said and, more importantly, know when they have not understood a verbal instruction (metacognition).   Also, it is largely up to the child to know how to resolve problems of incomprehension by, for instance, asking appropriate questions. This area, known as **referential communication**, has been the subject of much research. Children are generally poor at evaluating ambiguous or inadequate messages when they arrive at school, probably because of the different status (the supportive nature, already mentioned) that language has enjoyed in the home (Robinson and Whittaker, 1986). What leads to improvement is still a matter of debate but one possibility is the acquisition of reading and writing skills.

FIGURE 25: Teachers are a powerful force in structuring the learning environment.

Reading and writing

Inevitably, literacy must feed into this process and Vygotsky emphasized the importance of what he called 'written speech'. A number of researchers (for example, Donaldson, 1978) have endorsed this. Donaldson's view is that the literate child is able to consider words in a way not previously available. Because they are 'frozen' on the page they can be reflected upon, something denied to us with the transient nature of ordinary speech. The opportunity to think about what we read and what we write is an important factor in helping to free, or disembed, our thinking from the immediate social and perceptual context. This new perspective on words and their underlying concepts impacts on language as a whole. Instead of seeing language as a transparent medium for expressing our intentions, it takes on a second, more opaque, property. During their early years in school, children begin to understand that language can be used to express propositions that may be true or false, clear or ambiguous, easy or difficult to comprehend.

SAQ
22

How do educational experiences involving language and literacy influence intellectual development?

Applications from an information processing perspective

The essence of the information processing approach is the emphasis on breaking an activity down into its component skills. This is a useful way of helping children who have difficulty in reading or with mathematics. It is important to know which particular cognitive processes are responsible for performance defects in say memory, attention and language. Let us look at one area, number.

Basic developments in number

Understanding of number (or quantity) begins early since even **neonates** (newborn infants) can discriminate between groups of dots of different size. Reliable judgements of actual number take longer to develop and depend on counting. This, in turn, is made up of three component skills:

1. Knowing the sequence of number words: one, two, three, etc.

2. Being able to match number words and objects being counted. (See Figure 26)

3. Knowing the relationship between counting and the total number of objects that are counted. Thus, when children have counted a set of beads, one to six, and are asked how many beads there are, they must know that the answer is 'six'.

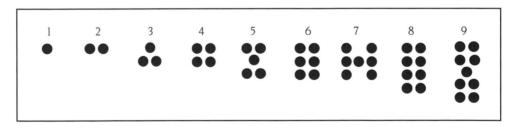

FIGURE 26: A number board such as this can help children understand the relationship between numerals and the number of countable objects that they stand for.

Counting can cause difficulty. Even straightforward counting can be problematic if you count any item more than once, or miss one out — watch a three-year-old counting aloud — but this skill is usually established by the time children start school at the age of five. Activities like pointing, using fingers and moving objects as they are counted, all help.

The significance of a simple activity, like counting, for arithmetic understanding is easily demonstrated. Addition is helped by processes like *counting-all* and *counting-on*. If you have to add 3 and 2, you use physical objects (for example, fingers) to represent the two entities and simply count all of them. Counting-on is more advanced: you start with one of the amounts, say *three*, and count on by two, that is, *four, five*. Later on, any external aid becomes unnecessary and we count in our heads. Later still, we can often dispense with counting altogether and retrieve the answer from memory.

The consensus emerging from research (Dockrell and McShane, 1993) is that most children develop many of their own counting strategies (that is, they are not taught) and that one strategy does not simply replace another. They may co-exist for long periods. It is also argued that it is unwise to suppress what might seem infantile behaviours among older children, such as counting on the fingers. Such strategies may be a sensible way to reduce demands on memory when doing mental arithmetic.

Language and mathematics

The world of number is not only about special notations and symbol manipulation. The point, for most of us, in learning about numbers at all is to use the knowledge in the real world. Take the following example from Dockrell and McShane (1993: 139).

> ▷ Mary went shopping for groceries. She spent £2.70 and had £2.30 left when she returned home. How much did she have when she left home?

This problem does not specify addition but this is what must be done to get the right answer. Children have trouble with problems of this sort and yet, typically, it is not the sum itself, nor a problem with the words themselves, which are straightforward enough. The difficulty seems to lie in equating the verbal statement with the mathematical representation. Difficulties can also arise from very simple words like *and*, *by*, *in*, *into*, *from*, and so on. Consider the following examples.

I went *by* bus.	Divide twelve *by* three.
I got *into* bed.	How many times does three go *into* twelve?
I came *from* home.	Take three *from* eight.

While we can see the similarity between the prepositions in the three pairs of sentences, it is not difficult to realize why they may cause young children to scratch their heads. It is the very familiarity of such terms, and verbs like *take*, *go* and *borrow*, that makes adjustment hard. Even statements like 'what are three and two' may seem strange to small children (Hughes, 1986), let alone 'Three into two won't go, so borrow ten'! It is another example of the general phenomenon referred to earlier with communication. Everyday language and thought ('embedded thinking' in Donaldson's terminology) is not always appropriate to learning situations like the classroom.

SAQ 23

What component skills are involved in being able to count properly? How do children use counting in their arithmetic?

Summary and conclusion

All the theories of cognitive development considered in this Unit are relevant to education. Piaget's theory has had the most widespread effect because of its influence on teacher training. In particular, the idea that children have active, enquiring minds that are capable of self-correction, and even self-instruction, is now generally accepted. A strict stage approach has less support but it is generally recognized that important conceptual shifts take place around six and twelve years of age.

The ideas of Bruner and Vygotsky are currently in vogue in the UK. Formal instruction is seen as a respectable component of teaching with language playing a dominant role. The idea that children respond to assistance, and can be helped to plan and regulate their own behaviour through sensitive tutoring, is accepted. And there is support for the mediating role of language. The broader impact of social influences on cognitive growth, such as group learning with peers and adults, is acknowledged by Piaget's as well as Vygotsky's followers. The difference mainly concerns causal mechanisms. Does change arise from the conflict of perspectives or through collaboration and agreement?

Information processing theory has its most telling effects on the curriculum. Research into the development of reading, writing, number and oral skills has used techniques and concepts derived from experimental cognitive psychology. As a result, a better understanding of the processes underlying the acquisition of basic school subjects is emerging. This is reflected in the ways in which standard methods of teaching are being pursued together with the diagnosis and treatment of **specific learning difficulties**.

The hopeful signs in this field are not only the breakthroughs that are being achieved in knowledge about language, literacy and number. More encouraging still is the recognition that it is unnecessary to argue for any one theoretical position at the expense of other standpoints. As Wood (1988) has shown, it is desirable to draw from all three positions and, in so doing, gain a richer and more secure understanding of how children think and learn.

SAQ
24

Give one example of a practical application of:
1. *Vygotsky's theory*
2. *Information processing theory*

REFERENCES

This list of references is included for the sake of completeness and for those planning further study or a project on the topics covered by this Unit. For most purposes, the books recommended in the Further Reading Section will be more than adequate.

ATKINSON, R.L., ATKINSON, R.C., SMITH, E.E. and BEM, D.J. (1993) *Introduction to Psychology, 11th edition*. Fort Worth, Texas: Harcourt Brace.

BARON-COHEN, S., LESLIE, A.M. and FRITH, U. (1985) Does the autistic child have a 'theory of mind'? *Cognition, 21,* 37—46.

BATES, E. (1976) *Language and Context*. New York: Academic Press.

BLOOM, L. (1970) *Language Development: Form and Function in Emerging Grammars*. Cambridge, Mass: MIT Press.

BRAINE, M. (1963) On learning the grammatical order of words. *Psychological Review, 70,* 323—48.

BROWN, R. (1973) *A First Language: the Early Stages*. London: Allen and Unwin.

BROWN, R., CAZDEN, C. and BELLUGI, U. (1969) The child's grammar from I to III. In J.P. Hill (Ed.) *Minnesota Symposium on Child Psychology, vol 2*. Minneapolis: University of Minnesota Press.

BRUNER, J.S. (1972) The nature and uses of immaturity. *American Psychologist, 27,* 687—708.

BRUNER, J.S. (1973) Organization of early skilled action. *Child Development, 44,* 1—11.

BRUNER, J.S. (1976) From communication to language — a psychological perspective. *Cognition, 3,* 225—287.

CLARK, E. (1973) Non-linguistic strategies and the acquisition of word meaning. *Cognition, 2,* 161—82.

CURTISS, S. (1977) *Genie: A Psycholinguistic Study of a Modern-day Wild Child*. New York: Academic Press.

DOCKRELL, J. and McSHANE, J. (1993) *Children's Learning Difficulties: A Cognitive Approach*. Oxford: Blackwell.

DAMON, W. (1977) *The Social World of the Child*. San Francisco: Jossey-Bass.

DONALDSON, M.C. (1978) *Children's Minds*. Glasgow: Fontana.

EDWARDS, D. and MERCER, N. (1987) *Common Knowledge*. London: Methuen.

EIMAS, P. (1985) The perception of speech in early infancy. *Scientific American, 252,* 46—52.

GELMAN, R. and SPELKE, E. (1981) The development of thoughts about animate and inanimate objects: Implications for research on social cognition. In J.H. Flavell and L. Ross (Eds.) *Social Cognitive Development*. New York: Cambridge University Press.

HIRSH-PASEK, K., TREIMAN, R. and SCHNEIDERMAN, M. (1984) Brown and Hanlon revisited: Mothers' sensitivity to ungrammatical forms. *Journal of Child Language, 11,* 81—88.

HOFF-GINSBERG, E. (1986) Function and structure in maternal speech: their relation to the child's development of syntax. *Developmental Psychology, 22,* 155—163.

HUGHES, M. (1986) *Children and Number*. Oxford: Blackwell.

KEENEY, T.J., CANNIZZO, S.R. and FLAVELL, J.H. (1967) Spontaneous and induced verbal rehearsal in a recall task. *Child Development, 38,* 953—66.

KENISTON, A.H. and FLAVELL, J.H. (1979) A developmental study of intelligent retrieval. *Child Development, 50,* 1144—1152.

KUCZAJ, S.A. (1977) The acquisition of regular and irregular past tense forms. *Journal of Verbal Learning and Verbal Behaviour, 16,* 589—600.

LENNEBERG, E. (1969) On explaining language. *Science, 164,* 635—643.

LIGHT, P. and BUTTERWORTH, G. (1992) *Context and Cognition: Ways of Learning and Knowing*. Hemel Hempstead, Harvester Wheatsheaf.

LLOYD, P. (1982) Talking to some purpose. In M.C. Beveridge (Ed.) *Children Thinking Through Language*. London: Edward Arnold.

McNEILL, D. (1970) *The Acquisition of Language: The Study of Developmental Psycholinguistics*. New York: Harper and Row.

McSHANE, J. (1991) *Cognitive Development: An Information Processing Approach*. Oxford: Blackwell.

MARKMAN, E. M. (1979) Realizing that you don't understand: elementary school children's awareness of inconsistencies. *Child Development, 50,* 643—55.

MILLER, G.A. (1956) The magical number seven, plus or minus two: some limits on our capacity for processing information. *Psychological Review, 63,* 81—97.

NELSON, K. (1973) Structure and strategy in learning to talk. *Monographs of the Society for Research in Child Development, 38,* serial no: 149.

NEWPORT, E.L.(1990) Maturational constraints on language learning. *Cognitive Science, 14,* 11—28.

NINIO, A. and BRUNER, J.S. (1978) The achievements and antecedents of labelling. *Journal of Child Language, 5,* 1—15.

O'BRIEN, K.G. and BOERSMA, F.J. (1971) Eye movements, perceptual activity and conservation development. *Journal of Experimental Child Psychology, 12,* 157—69.

PERNER, J., LEEKHAM, S., and WIMMER, H. (1987) Three-year-olds' difficulty with false belief: the case for a conceptual deficit. *British Journal of Developmental Psychology, 5,* 125—37.

PIAGET, J. (1971) *The Science of Education and the Psychology of the Child*. London: Longman.

THE PLOWDEN REPORT (1967) *Children and their Primary Schools*. London: Central Advisory Council for Education.

ROBINSON, E. and WHITTAKER, S. (1986) Learning about referential communication in the early school years. In K. Durkin (Ed.) *Language Development in the School Years*. Beckenham, Kent: Croom-Helm.

SIEGLER, R (1978) The origins of scientific reasoning. In R.S. Siegler (Ed.) *Children's Thinking: What Develops?* Hillsdale, NJ: Erlbaum.

SLOBIN, D.I. (1973) Cognitive prerequisites for the development of grammar. In C. Ferguson and D. Slobin (Eds.) *Studies of Child Language Development*. New York: Holt, Rinehart & Winston.

THARP, R AND GALLIMORE, R. (1988) *Rousing Minds to Life*. Cambridge: Cambridge University Press.

SNOW, C. (1977) The development of conversation between mothers and babies. *Journal of Child Language*, 4, 1—22.

TREVARTHEN, C. (1978) Communication and cooperation in early infancy. In M. Bullowa (Ed.) *Before Speech*, Cambridge: Cambridge University Press.

VYGOTSKY, L. (1978) Mind and Society: *The Development of Higher Psychological Processes*. Cambridge, Mass: Harvard University Press.

WERTSCH, J.V., McNAMEE, G.D., McLANE, J.B. and BUDWIG, N.A. (1980) The adult-child dyad as a problem-solving system. *Child Development*, 51, 1215—1221.

WIMMER, H. and PERNER, J. (1983) Beliefs about beliefs: representations and constraining function of wrong beliefs in young children's understanding of deception. *Cognition*, 13, 103—128 .

WOOD, D. (1988) *How Children Think and Learn*. Oxford: Blackwell.

FURTHER READING

BUTTERWORTH, G. and HARRIS, M. (1994) *Principles of Developmental Psychology*. Hove: Erlbaum. [Aimed at A-level and other beginners to psychology, this provides useful introductions to Piaget and Vygotsky as well as discussing central issues like nature/nurture. There is also a chapter on language development.]

CRAIN, W. (1992) *Theories of Development*. 3rd Edition. Englewood Cliffs, NJ: Prentice Hall [Good chapters on Piaget, Vygotsky and Chomsky.]

CRYSTAL, D. (1986) *Listen to your Child*. Harmondsworth: Penguin [Called a Parent's Guide to Children's Language, David Crystal offers an informative and entertaining account of what is known about language development. Full of amusing examples and ideas for mini-projects.]

DONALDSON, M. (1978) *Children's Minds*. London: Fontana. [Addressed to a lay audience this has become a classic. It provides a highly readable account of mental growth in the first ten years informed by the research of Margaret Donaldson and her colleagues in Edinburgh. Contains constructive criticism of Piaget.]

HIGGINS, L. (1988) *Learning to talk*. Leicester: BPS books (British Psychological Society). [A twenty minute audio cassette and booklet tracing the development of language from birth to three.]

PIAGET, J. and INHELDER, B. (1969) *The Psychology of the Child*. London: Routledge. [The most accessible book written by Piaget and his long time associate. It provides a complete account of Piaget's theory and approach in 150 pages. At the same time it is not an easy read but it will give you a flavour of how Piaget tackled the problem of intellectual development.]

WOOD, D. (1988) *How Children Think and Learn*. Oxford: Blackwell. [Written principally with teachers in mind, David Wood draws together the contributions of Piaget, Vygotsky, Bruner and information processing theory to provide a convincing account of cognitive development.]

VYGOTSKY, L. (1962) *Thought and Language*. Cambridge, Mass: MIT Press. [A Seminal Work.]

Other Open Learning Units of direct relevance in the same series are:

CASSELLS, A. (1991) *Remembering and Forgetting*. Leicester: BPS books (British Psychological Society)

CASSELLS, A. and GREEN, P. (1991) *Perception*. Leicester: BPS books (British Psychological Society)

HARTLAND, J. (1991) *Language and Thought*. Leicester: BPS books (British Psychological Society)

ANSWERS TO SELF-ASSESSMENT QUESTIONS

SAQ 1 1: Bruner; 2: Vygotsky; 3: Information processing 4: Piaget.

SAQ 2 Assimilation is where the child incorporates new information to fit existing ways of dealing with the world. Accommodation is the complementary process of adapting to the demands which the world of objects and events imposes on us.

SAQ 3 Any three of the five features listed on page 5 are appropriate.

SAQ 4 An eighteen-month-old will have little, if any, language and its motor skills are not fully developed. Its mental world is very limited. Any games, therefore, have to be directed largely by the adult. These will be simple games like 'giving and taking an object' and 'building and knocking over a pile of bricks'. In contrast, the three-year-old is a talking and thinking person who can imitate activities, express needs, take part in pretend games, draw, enjoy stories and name objects in picture books.

SAQ 5 The fact that Sam can name his brother (George) but does not realize that George must, therefore, also have a brother (Sam himself) is indicative of Sam's egocentrism or lack of reversibility in his thinking. He sees the relationship, brother, as one-way and thus fails to appreciate its reciprocal nature — to be a brother you have to have a brother (or sister).

SAQ 6 Conservation refers to the identity of objects. Properties like amount and length do not change simply because you rearrange the order of things or change, in some other way, the surface form. Young children lack the logical capacity to conserve identity (such as a given amount of Plasticine), across irrelevant transformations (such as rolling it from a ball into a sausage shape).

SAQ 7 Formal operational thinking corresponds to logical and scientific ways of solving problems rather than a haphazard, trial-and-error approach. Verbal and abstract problems can be assessed for their truth and falsity, and the future can be contemplated and new ideas hypothesized and tested.

SAQ 8 The ZPD may be seen as a mental potential carried by all of us, which represents competence that will only be demonstrated when we collaborate with someone else. Thus a child may be able to display very little skill at solving a crossword but when given some help, such as prompts, or other ways of thinking about the clues, a much better level of performance is revealed.

SAQ 9 Egocentrism is a term mainly associated with Piaget. It refers to a characteristic of children's thinking, especially during the pre-operational stage, in which perspectives, both literal and conceptual, are always from the standpoint of the viewer. It represents, therefore, a highly blinkered approach to the world and results in inflexible and, indeed, fallacious thinking. Vygotsky used the term in a more positive sense as applied to language. Egocentric speech was, for Vygotsky, the precursor of regulative speech, that is internal speech that can guide thinking. For Piaget, egocentric speech was an outward manifestation of the child's inability to engage in effective dialogue. By and large, Piaget's strong position on egocentric speech has not prevailed and egocentrism has been shown to be influenced by the way in which tasks are presented.

SAQ 10 1: Piaget; 2: Vygotsky; 3: Vygotsky; 4: Piaget; 5: Piaget; 6: Vygotsky.

SAQ 11 1. Enactive 2. Iconic and symbolic 3. Symbolic 4. Symbolic 5. Symbolic and iconic 6. Symbolic and iconic 7. Enactive and iconic. (You may have arrived at one or two different answers which are not necessarily wrong. The above choices should be regarded as the main modes of representation. Others are not precluded.)

SAQ 12 'Scaffolding' refers to the support given by adults (typically caregivers) in their activities with children. It can be seen in nursery games such as peep-bo (which Bruner called 'formats') where the game would not happen unless the adult put in considerable effort. It is also seen in early dialogues between parent and child. It can be considered part of the zone of proximal development although scaffolding does not have the formal properties of ZPD.

SAQ 13 Processing strategies refer to ways of making better use of your cognitive capacity such as repeating things to yourself (rehearsal) in order to remember them. Elaboration and systematic searching are other examples of processing strategies. Rule-based strategies are revealed in children's problem solving such as those uncovered by Siegler in his balance scale experiment. The difference, therefore, is that processing strategies are procedures that gradually, with age, become automatic ways of dealing more effectively with information. Rule-based strategies are higher level, knowledge based, approaches to problem solving that also change with age and follow Piaget's account of cognitive development quite closely. They tend to be context dependent and do not have the permanency of processing strategies.

SAQ 14 'Human sense' refers to the extent to which situations used in psychological tasks with children relate to their everyday understanding. Children find it easier to take the perspective of another, for example, in situations they can easily relate to — like hiding from someone else — than a more formal problem like the three mountains task. It has been found that changing features of Piagetian tasks to make them closer to human sense can lead to improved performance (see Donaldson, 1978).

SAQ 15 Theory of mind refers to someone's ability to attribute a state of mind to another person. What does another person believe, for example, in a particular circumstance? It has been found that five-year-olds are able to distinguish what they themselves know (a true belief) from what another may know (a false belief) because some intervening event has taken place. For example, if two children both see a marble placed in a basket and then one of them leaves the room and the marble is taken from the basket and put in a box, the five-year-old will say that when their friend returns she will look for the marble in the basket. Three-year-olds, in contrast, will credit the friend with their own knowledge and say that she will look in the box. Three-year-olds, therefore, have an undeveloped theory of mind which fails to recognize that their friend actually holds a false belief about the location of the marble.

SAQ 16 1. One is *rich interpretation* which gives a greater role to context — linguistic and non-linguistic — in order to understand what the child is saying.
2. A second is the increasing concern with language as communication; the nature of the input; language as it is used rather just its formal syntactic and semantic properties.

SAQ 17 The sudden growth in vocabulary tends to coincide with the beginning of two-word combinations which, in itself, would lead to acceleration. The advance in internal representation which comes towards the end of the sensorimotor period would facilitate this growth. Bruner also points to the role played by caregivers through such activities as book reading.

SAQ 18 This is a big question. Briefly, children may have both narrower and broader meanings for words than adults. For example, one child may use the word 'kitty' to refer solely to their own cat while another word, like 'car', may be applied to many different vehicles, some inappropriately. Relational words, like 'more' and 'less', are understood in a much fuzzier way by children. They will often use them interchangeably and responses can be determined by non-linguistic preferences such as opting for the larger, more salient amount, whether asked for more or less.

SAQ 19 Any three of the following:
1. Words tend to lack inflections.
2. Articles ('the', 'a') and other function words (e.g. prepositions) are omitted.
3. Sentences are usually in the present tense, ignoring past and future.
4. Utterances are short and telegraphic.
5. Two-word utterances can be reduced to two classes: *pivot* — a modifying category — and *open*, a large group, typically nouns, that can fit into a slot alongside a single pivot.

SAQ 20 A critical period is an interval of time during which development is likely to suffer if the child is deprived of appropriate stimulation. If a child does not grow up in a normal language community, beyond a certain age the chances of ever using language normally are slight. The best evidence comes from studies of deaf people. The critical period for learning sign language seems to be birth to four years. Children starting after that time never achieve the mastery of earlier starters.

SAQ 21 Teachers have been influenced by the idea that knowledge is acquired through the child's own active discovery of lawful relationships in the world. In addition, the idea that development is brought about by optimal conflict between what the child already knows and what is to be known, has challenged teachers to create learning environments that offer such opportunities.

SAQ 22 The evidence for the influence of literacy on cognitive development is largely lacking but the idea has been put forward that literacy encourages a more reflective form of thinking. This is because when we read and write we can continue to consider the words that are in front of us in a way that is not possible with ephemeral spoken language. The language used in the classroom is different from that used in the home and playground. It focuses on different subject matter and it lacks the supportive framework found in the home. Because of this, the child comes to realize that language has other properties such as truth and falsity, clarity and ambiguity. This, in turn, gradually leads to a more efficient way of processing verbal information.

SAQ 23 First of all, counting requires knowledge of the number line: one, two, three, etc. Then you must know that all items must be included, but once only, and that the last number you count represents the total number in the group. In arithmetic, children use procedures like 'counting-all' to do sums like 3 + 2, thus counting, say, all five fingers. 'Counting-on' is when you start at one number, say three, and count on by two: four, five. Recent research suggests we should not suppress children's 'primitive' counting strategies since they help to reduce processing demands when doing mental arithmetic.

SAQ 24 1. The idea that children can be taken from one level of understanding to a new higher level through carefully planned programmes of instruction owes much to Vygotsky's notion of the zone of proximal development. Any teaching procedure which stresses social interaction and mediation by language may be derived from Vygotsky's theory.
2. The emphasis on breaking down learning activities into their component skills is typical of the IP approach. The example of counting and arithmetic, referred to in the previous SAQ, is one such example. Similar progress has also been made in the field of reading.

Illustration credits:

Box 1. Helen Welford
Fig.1, © John K. Blay, Barnaby's Picture Library;
Fig.3, © H. R. Hood, Barnaby's Picture Library;
Fig.6. Helen Welford
Fig.13, © Frazer Wood, Barnaby's Picture Library;
Fig.16, © Bob Bray, Barnaby's Picture Library;
Fig.19. Helen Welford
Fig.21, © V. Blissland, Barnaby's Picture Library;
Fig.24, © Bob Bray, Barnaby's Picture Library;
Fig.25, © Leslie Howling, Barnaby's Picture Library.

GLOSSARY

Terms within the text in bold type also appear as a seperate entry

Accommodation: Piaget's term referring to the way in which modes of thinking may be modified according to the demands placed on mental structures by the environment. See also **adaptation** and **assimilation.**

Adaptation: Piaget's term for the cognitive processes through which a person adjusts to new ideas or experience. Adaptation takes two forms, **assimilation** and **accommodation.**

Assimilation: Piaget's term referring to the way in which new information is incorporated into existing mental structures. See also **adaptation** and **accommodation.**

Autism: a serious psychological disorder of early childhood in which a child fails to make normal social contact and therefore reflected in communication and other social behaviours.

Automatized: in cognitive terms, thought underlying action that is so well learned or practised that it is carried out without awareness and without apparent effort.

Babbling: vocal play by young infants; typically as extended repetition of vowel-consonant pairs (ba-ba-ba) beginning at about five months.

Behaviourism: theory that states that psychologists should study observable behaviour rather than try to infer inner mental states.

Chain complexes: a stage in Vygotsky's account of children's thinking in which concepts are formed according to surface features which the child switches between haphazardly. There is no consistent underlying 'formal' property.

Concept: an idea, especially abstract. For example, with the concept of 'dogs' the reference is to dogs in general rather than a particular dog.

Concrete operational period: in Piaget's theory the third period of cognitive development starting at about six years; characterized by the development of logical thinking about concrete events and experiences, but not hypothetical or abstract ones.

Conservation: the realization that the essential identity of something does not change because surface appearance is altered. For example, the length of a piece of wire does not alter because it is bent into an S-shape. According to Piaget, conservation depends on the presence of logical thinking and is, therefore, absent at the pre-operational stage of development.

Constructivist theory: often used to apply to Piaget's theory and referring to the way in which children actively construct for themselves their understanding of the world.

Critical period: an interval of time during which certain physical or psychological growth must occur if development is to proceed normally.

Decentering: the process of simultaneously focusing on more than one aspect of a situation at a time; includes the ability to consider another's point of view. The opposite of centering and **egocentrism.**

Determinist: a view of behaviour as being rigidly influenced by the external forces present in the environment.

Domain: a particular cognitive discipline or focus of activity, e.g. spatial reasoning, computer knowledge.

Egocentrism: thinking that is fixated from the point of view of the individual alone. According to Piaget, a principal feature of preoperational thought.

Enactive representation: knowledge that is represented and also expressed in the form of motor routines. Coined by Bruner, it refers to the earliest mode of cognitive representation.

Empirical: the belief that something is answerable on the basis of evidence or experiment.

Encoding: the placing of information into memory or the process of constructing a verbal message.

Equilibration: the term used by Piaget for the back-and-forth process of seeking a balance between existing psychological structures and new environmental circumstances. It is akin to responding to a disturbance in the system. When a balance is achieved, between **accommodation** and **assimilation**, cognitive development ensues.

Executive: a hypothetical notion referring to a decision-making and monitoring centre in the cognitive system; one that has overall control over the distribution of information processing capacities.

False belief: a belief that was once true becomes false when circumstances change. The ability of children who know about a changed situation to attribute a false belief to a person who is unaware of the change is one of the principal ways of assessing a theory of mind.

Formal operation: in Piaget's theory the mental ability acquired in adolescence enabling abstract logical thinking and the ability to plan and speculate about the future. Formal operations include hypothetico-deductive, inductive and reflective thinking.

Formats: the term Bruner uses to refer to activities like games of peekaboo and bedtime routines between young children and their caregivers. These socially patterned events are thought to be important precursors to more complex activity like verbal communication.

Iconic representation: a term used by Bruner to refer to a mode of thinking that is identical or very similar to that which it stands for, such as images.

Inflections: word endings such as -ing, -ed, 's.

Information handling techniques: procedures by which incoming sensory information is dealt with efficiently. Such techniques develop with age and call upon existing cognitive capacity in the realm of memory, attention, etc.

Internalization: can be viewed as a process or state. The act or state of having internal mental ways of viewing or thinking about things, such as inner speech and images.

Introspection: a school of psychology that holds that the accessible contents of one's mental life are valuable evidence for a scientific understanding of the mind.

Language Acquisition Device (LAD): because language is acquired so rapidly and apparently so effortlessly by children, at a time when other cognitive achievements are limited, it was proposed that there must be an innate (in-built) device to facilitate this accomplishment. First postulated by Chomsky, it became known as the Language Acquisition Device.

Lexicon: a person's available set of words or vocabulary.

Markers: linguistic terms or inflections which usually signal a change of meaning, e.g. 'not', '-ed'.

Maturation: developmental change that is controlled by hereditary timing mechanisms.

Mediating processes: mental processes, such as language and thought, that influence behaviour.

Metacognition: the awareness of one's own cognitive processes.

Modifiers: a word which affects the interpretation of another word or word combination, such as an adjective.

Nature: the belief that behaviour and development are influenced primarily by hereditary factors.

Neonate: a newborn baby; up to one month of age.

Nonsense word: a word having no meaning such as, for English, 'miv'. They have been used in experimental studies of memory in an attempt to remove semantic and other associations.

Nurture: the idea that behaviour and development are controlled primarily by environmental influences.

Object permanence: the understanding that objects continue